GUGA

BREAKING THE BARBECUE RULES

GUGA

BREAKING THE BARBECUE RULES

GUSTAVO TOSTA

Publisher Mike Sanders
Art & Design Director William Thomas
Senior Editor Brook Farling
Assistant Director of Art & Design Rebecca Batchelor
Photographer (Miami) Leo Diaz
Food Stylist (Miami) Frankie Chacon
Photographer (Indianapolis) Lovoni Walker
Food Stylist (Indianapolis) Lovoni Walker
Recipe Tester Thomas England
Proofreaders Lisa Himes, Lisa Starnes
Indexer Brad Herriman

First American Edition, 2023
Published in the United States by DK Publishing
DK, a Division of Penguin Random House LLC
6081 E. 82nd Street, Suite 400, Indianapolis, IN 46250

The authorized representative in the EEA is Dorling Kindersley
Verlag GmbH. Arnulfstr. 124, 80636 Munich, Germany

Library of Congress Catalog Number: 2022941352
ISBN 978-0-7440-6080-5

DK books are available at special discounts when purchased in
bulk for sales promotions, premiums, fund-raising, or
educational use.
For details, contact: SpecialSales@dk.com.

Printed and bound in China

For the curious
www.dk.com

This book was made with Forest
Stewardship Council ™ certified
paper – one small step in DK's
commitment to a sustainable future.
For more information go to
www.dk.com/our-green-pledge

DEDICATION

I would like to dedicate this book to my mother. She is the one who pushed me to be a better person, inspired me to be positive, and most importantly, taught me to be creative and kind to others. Mãe, I am forever indebted to you. May you shine in Heaven like you did here on Earth. We love you forever.

ACKNOWLEDGMENTS

I would not be who I am today without my amazing wife. Thank you for being there every step of the way, pushing me to do better, and believing in me even when I didn't.

Thank you to my three children for keeping me young and motivating me to learn the new slang; you are my whole life.

To my family here in the United States and in Brazil, thank you for teaching me that being a good person is the most important thing in life. Family is number one and will always be number one.

Thanks to the Guga Team; Michael Gordon and the team at Night Media; my meat dealer, Emilio; and Brook and the DK team, for all your amazing work and for helping this book become a reality.

A HUGE thank you to my awesome viewers, followers, and subscribers! You keep me going! I take inspiration from your comments and suggestions and enjoy making them become a reality. We have built an amazing cooking community, and I love you forever!

CONTENTS

EXTRAS 155

SIDES & APPETIZERS 171

SAUCES, RUBS & SEASONINGS . . . 199

HELLO, EVERYBODY!

If you know me, you know I love to cook for my family and friends. One of the best feelings I can get is when I see the happy reactions whenever I break the traditional rules of cooking and discover new and amazing ways to get phenomenal results. I am humbled that you are holding this book in your hands, and I hope that through these recipes you can feel the same joy I feel when someone takes that first bite of something delicious I've just cooked.

And when I say "break the rules," sometimes it means I really try to break the rules. Combining peanut butter and steak? Sure, why not?! Combining steak and Nutella? Well, maybe not! Either way, I want to share with you the bliss I always feel when I'm experimenting with different flavors and cooking techniques. I can't wait to share what's in these pages and show you that you don't have to be intimidated by a grill or a smoker, and you can cook some amazing food that will really impress your friends and family. I want to inspire you to forget the rules and find freedom and creativity in your cooking.

I truly hope you enjoy my recipes, but I don't want you to feel bound by them. Once you become comfortable making a dish, don't be afraid to add an ingredient here or there to make the recipes your own. There are no rules here! You'll find out quickly that you can do some amazing things with just a few simple ingredients, a nice juicy steak, and some fire! So take out your grill, flip through the pages of this book, find a recipe that inspires you, and let me show you how easy and fun it is to cook and eat like a king (or a queen)!

Now enough talking! Let's do it!

Guga

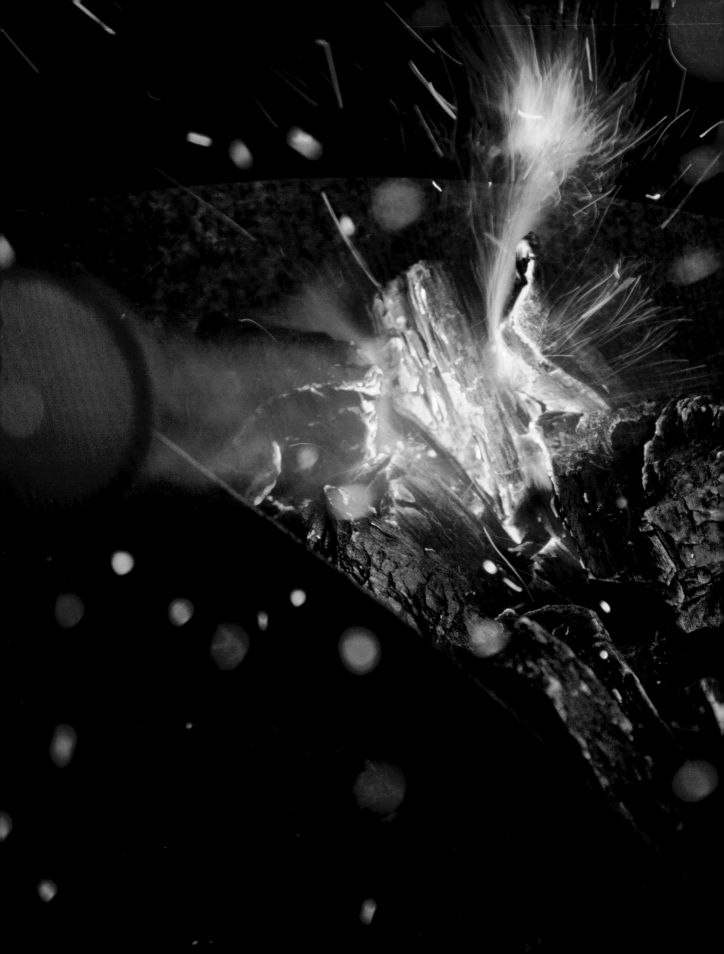

LET'S ROCK AND ROLL

MEET GUGA

Guga (aka Gustavo Tosta) is one of the most popular social media cooks on the internet. In addition to having channels on TikTok and Instagram, he is the creative force behind three massively popular YouTube channels: *Guga Foods, Sous Vide Everything,* and *Guga.*

For Guga, there are no rules when it comes to cooking. He's not afraid to challenge traditional cooking beliefs and experiment with unorthodox ideas. One of the reasons Guga is so popular is that he's not afraid to share both his failures and his successes with his followers. And his mouthwatering dishes have the magical ability to stop mindless scrolling and turn his followers' afternoons into cooking marathons!

Guga's personal story is one that is rich in diversity. He was born in Brazil and came to the United States at a very young age. As a kid, he went to school in Miami, Florida, and eventually developed a passion for martial arts. Guga eventually became a taekwondo master and instructor, and it's through this practice that he developed his ability to teach people of all ages how to learn in a very logical and organized manner, and that skill subsequently translated into how he teaches his followers how to cook. Guga eventually transitioned to a successful career in web design and development, but he quickly realized his true passion was cooking, and that's what eventually set him on the path to becoming one of the world's most recognized steak experts.

Guga now lives in the melting pot that is Miami, Florida, where he has access to an incredibly diverse mix of cultures and cooking traditions. He is a family man, and his videos are centered around the overwhelmingly loving relationship he has with his family. His sidekicks in most of the videos are also his family... and now you are too.

GRILLS

Grills are the same as cars or wristwatches: a cheap car will get you from point A to point B the same way an expensive car will, and a five-dollar wristwatch will still tell time. My point is that you don't need the most expensive grill or the fanciest smoker to cook amazing food. In my opinion, a kettle grill and a pellet smoker will do everything you need, and they both will do it at an affordable price. But if you're insane like me and love to cook, you just might want to have a different type of grill or smoker for every type of recipe! There are lots of different types of grills to choose from, and some are better for some things than for others. It all depends on your budget and how fancy you want to get.

KETTLE GRILL

A kettle grill is what I use most because of its versatility. You can use it as a regular charcoal grill, but you can also toss in some wood chunks and use it as a smoker. A kettle grill cooks hot and fast, but it can also cook low and slow. I've used a kettle grill to cook very large slabs of meat and also to cook delicate cuts of meat. It works really well for any kind of cook and that's why it's one of my favorites. It also gives you the biggest bang for your buck!

KAMADO GRILL

A kamado grill is getting into big-boy territory in terms of usage and price. This type of grill is made of a ceramic material that retains heat really well. That means you'll use less charcoal or wood when you're cooking. This style of grill is perfect for grilling steaks or smoking a big brisket, but no matter what you decide to cook on it, it will get the job done well. Yes, it might be a bit more expensive than a kettle grill, but trust me when I say it's definitely worth every penny if you can afford it.

GAS GRILL

I'm going to be honest, I don't use a gas grill and I don't really like them, but I know a lot of you have them and love them, so I wanted to make sure the recipes in this book will work for gas grills as well. Many people own them because they're convenient— all you need to do is turn on the gas, light up the grill, and start grilling, but to me it's almost no different than using your stove.

Kettle grill

Gas grill

ROTISSERIE GRILL

This is another grill that is getting into big-boy price territory. This grill is great if you're throwing parties and making food for lots of people. The fact that the meat is on a rotisserie and constantly turning allows you to cook many types of meat at the same time, but this grill is not the best option for the everyday home cook.

FLAT TOP GRILL

A flat top grill has a direct heat source (most commonly gas) underneath the cooking surface, which heats up the cooking surface, allowing you to cook right on top of it. This type of grill is good if you're cooking multiple things at once, like fried rice or a big breakfast, but it's not the same as a grill when it comes to cooking. It's not going to impart that nice charcoal flavor that we all love, but it can get the job done for lots of foods. Bottom line: it's like a big cast-iron skillet!

CAJA CHINA GRILL

This kind of grill works amazingly well for one thing and is horrible for practically everything else. This is my go-to grill when I'm cooking an entire pork roast. But I wouldn't even consider using it for anything else! The amount of maintenance and work that goes into it can take up an entire day. Shoveling charcoal and making sure the heat is even throughout the grill is a lot of work. But if you're willing to put in the work and you cook pork often, this might be a good option.

With that said, you should use what is best for you, especially if it will enable you to cook outdoors and create memories with your family and friends. That is what cooking is all about!

WOOD FIRE GRILL

A wood fire grill is a bit more expensive than a charcoal grill and also much larger. It also requires a lot of maintenance during cooking; this is not the type of grill that you can just set it and forget it. You have to be constantly watching the fire and making sure the temperature of the grill is correct for the cook. But the flavor this type of grill produces is almost impossible to replicate with a charcoal grill. These are so much fun to use, and they last a long time. Just remember that they do cost a pretty penny, and they do require attention!

ELECTRIC GRILL

In my opinion, this is the worst kind of grill you can buy. You're better off just using your indoor stove, which is pretty much the same thing! For even more money you can get an infrared electric grill, but it still works just okay. If you're considering this option, save your money and get a kettle grill or kamado grill.

SMOKERS

There are several different types of smokers you can purchase, depending on your budget and what types of features you want. You can always use a kettle grill as a basic smoker, but if you want to up your game, these are both great options.

PELLET SMOKER

A pellet smoker might not be the least expensive option, but it definitely is one of the most convenient. You can cook almost anything in a pellet smoker, and you don't have to worry about using real wood or watching the smoker constantly to make sure the flames aren't getting too big. You pretty much can just set it and forget it since it keeps an accurate temperature. It also imparts that awesome smoky flavor to whatever you're cooking, which is always a plus in my book!

DRUM SMOKER

A drum smoker uses charcoal as a fuel source and wood chunks to add smoke flavor. It's a better option than a kettle grill when it comes to smoking because of the intense flavor it can add to meat, even if you don't use wood and only use charcoal. However, they are not as good when it comes to grilling because the heat source is so low in the drum. To grill, you need the heat source to be close to the meat. But to be honest, I really do love these things!

BBQ TOOLS & EQUIPMENT

Here are some of the essential tools and equipment that you'll need as you begin to cook the recipes in this book. Some of these are must-haves while others are just nice to have.

FLAMETHROWER

Not all outdoor cooking tools are necessary to have, but if there is one that I would say is necessary, it's the flamethrower. I use it every day! It has multiple uses: it can help you start the fire by igniting the coals or wood, and it can also put a beautiful crust on a steak. If you like to cook outdoors, this tool is a must-have. Plus, it makes you look like a badass!

TONGS

Tongs are simple, convenient, and another must-have tool. They allow you to maneuver meat around the grill or smoker while still staying safely away from the fire. They come in both inexpensive and expensive versions, but you should avoid the fancy ones, they are not worth the money; just stick with the cheap stuff. Look for lightweight tongs that are inexpensive, and avoid any that have wood handles. You will want to have multiple tongs on hand, both long and short.

GLOVES

There are two types of heat gloves I use. The first type is the thicker oven gloves. They're not good for handling meat, but I still use them to pick up hot trays or take things out of the oven. The second type is a bit thinner and doesn't hold heat as well as oven gloves. I use those to move meat in and out of the smoker. Both are very good to have, but each has a different use. (Make sure to put some powder-free latex gloves over them before using either type of glove.) Nitrile gloves that are food grade and powder free are good for handling raw meat to ensure everything stays clean. Avoid poly plastic gloves; they tear easily and can melt if you are handling hot foods.

BASTING BRUSH

This is a very basic tool that is helpful when basting steaks and other meats. The most important thing about a good basting brush is that it's long so that you are not too close to the fire when you're basting. You'll want to have a brush with heat-resistant silicone bristles so the bristles don't burn when they make contact with the flames.

KNIVES

If you know me, you know I have too many knives to count! But in reality, all you need are three knives: a boning knife, a chef's knife, and a slicing knife. A boning knife is shorter and allows you to make more precise cuts; it's mostly used to remove bones from big cuts of meat. A chef's knife can be used for everything from butchering, to boning, to slicing big cuts of meat. I recommend having one with an 8-inch to 9-inch (20cm to 23cm) blade. A slicing knife is longer, makes nice smooth cuts, and is what I use for slicing beautiful steaks and big cuts of meat. Don't go cheap on your knives—buy the best you can afford!

CUTTING BOARDS

Cutting boards are pretty simple. There is no right or wrong type—they all have the same purpose. But in my opinion, wooden boards are the best because they last longer than other materials, they feel better when I'm cutting steaks, and most importantly, they just look good!

FLAMETHROWER

BASTING BRUSH

TONGS

MEAT TENDERIZER

INSTANT-READ THERMOMETER

CHEF'S KNIFE

TRUSSING NEEDLE

MEAT SCRAPER

WIRELESS THERMOMETER

INSTANT-READ AND WIRELESS THERMOMETERS

A high-quality instant-read thermometer is a must-have. The one I use gives me an accurate temperature reading within one second! This is an important tool because you'll need to be able to tell what the meat temperature is at any point in your cook. Another must-have is a wireless thermometer that allows you to know what temperature the food is at any time, even when it's in the smoker.

MEAT SCRAPER

A meat scraper does exactly what it says: it's scrapes things like smashburgers from flat surfaces where you may not be able to use a spatula. You can invest in a more expensive meat scraper, but I simply use a good old-fashioned paint scraper that I bought at a hardware store.

TENDERIZER

Tenderizers come in different styles and sizes, but the most common tenderizer is the type that looks like a hammer. It has a spiked end on one side of the head. This spiked end is used to tenderize tougher cuts.

TRUSSING NEEDLE

A trussing needle can be really handy when you need to truss thick cuts, like a pork belly.

COOKING METHODS

There are several cooking methods used to prepare the recipes in this book. And while smoking and grilling are the primary methods, there are other methods that will add depth of flavor and textures that will take your cooking to an entirely different level!

SMOKING

Think of smoking as another way to add flavor to your food. You're not really using the smoke to cook the food; you're still using heat to cook, but the smoke is like a seasoning, just like salt and pepper. And smoking isn't just for meats. You can smoke drinks, butters, fats, and other ingredients to give them all a fantastic smoky flavor. Smokers cook by holding a steady low-and-slow stream of heat that mixes with a little bit of water to create steam. If you don't have a smoker, you can still use a smoke gun, which enables you to add smoke flavor to virtually anything.

GRILLING

Direct grilling is used mostly for thin-cut steaks or other meats like fish that need to be cooked at high temperatures. The high temperature caramelizes the outside of the protein and gives it a crust, while not overcooking the middle of the protein. Indirect grilling is used for cooking thicker cuts of meat or thick-cut steaks that take a bit longer to cook. Indirect grilling ensures you don't burn the steak directly over the fire. This method is useful for getting meat to the right temperature. When you're ready to add the crust, you move it over the direct heat to get a quick sear.

SOUS VIDE

Sous vide is a method of cooking food in a water bath that has been set to a specific temperature. This process allows the heat from the water to cook the meat at a slower pace, reaching the perfect temperature every time. This means that there is no babysitting of the meat and it will never go over the set temperature; you simply set the sous vide machine and forget it. While this method isn't used for the recipes in this book, it's an incredible way to cook a steak. Once the steak is done cooking in the water bath, all you need to do is remove it from the water bath and place it on the grill to give it a nice sear.

DEEP-FRYING

Deep-frying involves dunking meat in hot oil until the meat is fully cooked. Since this method tends to cook foods very quickly, you have to watch the meat closely and remove it from the oil frequently to ensure you don't overcook it. Most people think that deep-frying is only used for meats like chicken, pork, and fish, but I use it for everything, even steak! There are many different fats you can use for deep-frying, including Wagyu, lard, chicken fat, bacon fat, clarified butter, and even cheese oil! Each will impart different flavors to the meat.

BAKING

Don't think that your grill is only good for grilling or searing. It's also good for baking! I've made several baked recipes on the grill, including mac and cheese, lasagna, bread, and even pizza. Your grill is not just a one-trick pony. With a little know-how and an experimental mind (like mine), a grill can be used for just about anything.

COOKING WITH CHARCOAL

Many people think charcoal is just a heat source for grilling or smoking. But if it's used properly, the smoke and aromas that are released from charcoal can be infused into the food you're cooking to have a similar effect of any type of seasoning you might otherwise use on the meat. I like to say that charcoal makes everything better!

COOKING LOW AND SLOW WITH CHARCOAL

Think about what happens when you sear a steak. Searing often needs to happen at temperatures above 500°F (260°C) in order to get the quickest possible sear on the steak. While a nice crust is added to the steak, almost no flavor from the charcoal is being imparted to the meat. What you do taste is the char produced by the sear, but not necessarily the flavor from the charcoal.

When you cook at lower temperatures over longer periods of time, flavor is added to the meat by the smoke and fumes that are produced when the fat of the steak drips onto the charcoal and then vaporizes. Can the same effect be achieved with a gas or propane grill? Not necessarily. Charcoal burns hotter than a gas grill. And its the vapors and smoke that come from cooking over charcoal that are unique to this style of outdoor cooking.

One of the reasons American-style barbecue is so amazing is the flavor that is produced through lower cooking temperatures and longer cooking times, both of which allow the smoke to penetrate and season the meat. Cooking temperatures between 225°F (107°C) and 275°F (135°C) are ideal for producing the greatest amount of flavor in meat.

GRILLING WITH A "CLEAN" FIRE

If you can't see smoke from the charcoal when you're grilling, that's actually a good thing. It means you are burning a "clean" fire. Just because you can't see smoke does not mean you are not imparting flavor to the meat. The juices and vapors from the meat will drip onto the coals and be infused into the meat, and that equals better flavor. If you are using a kettle grill, this might be a bit more difficult to achieve since the meat sits so close to the coals and can burn quickly. If you use a smoker, however, the meat is far enough away from the coals that it won't burn. But you get extra flavor as drippings from the meat hit the coals. To sum it up, if you can get drippings to hit the coals, cook at a low temperature, avoid flare-ups, and keep a steady temperature, your food will taste incredible!

CHOOSING YOUR FUEL

Briquettes are made of compressed wood. They work fine, but they don't impart as much flavor as lump charcoal, nor do they burn as hot as lump charcoal. They are cheaper than lump charcoal and easier to light. Lump charcoal is made of solid wood chunks. It burns hotter and longer than briquettes, but it's also more expensive than briquettes. The biggest advantage is flavor. In my opinion, lump charcoal has much better flavor than briquettes and is worth the money. Pellets are for pellet smokers and are made of compressed wood fibers. They come in a variety of "flavors" and are easy to use, but they can be a bit expensive.

STORING AND REUSING CHARCOAL

Charcoal should always be stored in a cool, dry environment where it's away from any sources of moisture or heat. Storing charcoal in a paper bag that has an outer plastic lining will work, but a proper charcoal storage container is a better option. Keeping it dry and away from sources of heat will ensure it's always ready to rock and roll when you're ready to cook. You can reuse once-burned lump charcoal, but it will produce less flavor than fresh charcoal. I like to use once-burned charcoal to sear meat, but if I'm cooking low and slow and need to impart flavor to the meat, I always use fresh, unburned charcoal.

Lump charcoal

Charcoal briquettes

Wood pellets

Wood

FIRE MANAGEMENT

Cooking with charcoal requires some patience and know-how in order to manage the heat levels and ensure you always get the results you want. Follow these steps and you'll be cooking like a pro in no time.

STEP 1: PREPARE THE GRILL

There are two primary methods of cooking on a grill: direct and indirect. Cooking over direct heat means you cook meats at a higher temperature, for less time, and directly over hot coals. Cooking over indirect heat means you cook meats at a lower temperature, for longer periods of time, and on an area of the grill that is not directly over hot coals. To achieve this, you'll want to use a **two-zone setup.** In a two-zone setup, charcoal is placed on only one side of the grill to create a direct-cooking zone. The area not directly over the charcoal is the indirect-cooking zone. This allows you to cook quickly at high temperatures over the direct-cooking zone, and also use the radiant heat from the coals to cook slower and at lower temperatures over the indirect zone because the meat is not directly over the coals. If you're cooking with gas, you can create a two-zone setup by leaving one or more burners off. While not every meat requires a two-zone setup, it's my preferred way to grill, particularly for steaks.

Two-zone setup

STEP 2: SET UP THE CHARCOAL

For low-temperature direct cooking, place a single, even layer of charcoal in the direct-cooking zone. For medium-temperature direct cooking, place a second, even layer of charcoal in the direct-cooking zone. For high-temperature direct cooking, add a third, even layer of charcoal or enough that the charcoal comes within 3 to 4 inches of the grill grate. If you're cooking burgers or meats that don't require a two-zone setup, you can cover the entire bottom surface of the grill using this same layering principle.

Low-temperature setup

Medium-temperature setup

High-temperature setup

To light the charcoal, you'll need a high-heat flame source. You can use a torch lighter, but I recommend using a flamethrower: it will light the charcoal in no time. You can also use a chimney starter, which will take a little more time than a flamethrower, but it will still get the job done. Remember: more charcoal means more heat! You'll want the charcoal to get really hot, which means the lumps should be white and not emitting any smoke. This will heat up the grates so they will sear meats like steaks quickly and allow the steaks to form a nice crust. Cooking on the indirect side will allow you to better control the cooking process and ensure you don't overcook the meat.

STEP 3: MANAGE THE TEMPERATURE

You can control the heat level in the grill by adjusting the vents to control the airflow and also by raising and lowering the grill grates (if your grill includes this feature). If your grill has a thermometer, you should be able to manage the temperature easily, but if you don't have a thermometer on your grill, you can still check the approximate heat level by holding your hand about 8 inches above the grill grates. For low heat (225°F–275°F [107°C–135°C]), you should be able to hold your hand above the heat for about 8 to 10 seconds before it feels too hot and you need to remove it. For medium heat (275°F–375°F [135°C–191°C]), you should be able to hold your hand above the heat for about 4 to 5 seconds. For high heat (375°F–500°F [191°C–260°C]), you should be able to hold your hand above the heat for only 1 to 2 seconds.

(Note that while placing your hand over a heat source is generally not recommended, this is how we did it in Brazil and how I still do it today. Just please be very careful if you use this method.)

GRILLING TECHNIQUES

Different types of meat and different cuts each require attenton to detail when you're grilling. What works for one type of meat may not work for another. Here are some simple tips for always getting the results you want.

Golden crust

THE MAILLARD REACTION

Many people have the misconception that grill marks on beef or pork cuts are an indication of a well-cooked cut. Grill marks are actually an indication that the surface of the meat has been charred and burned. What you actually want to create is a consistent golden-brown crust across the entire surface of the cut. The creation of this crust is called the *Maillard reaction,* and it occurs through the breakdown of sugars and proteins when they're introduced to heat. The last thing you want is for your steak to turn black or to form grill marks. What you're looking for is a nice golden-brown color on both sides.

GETTING THAT GOLDEN CRUST

The first trick for getting a perfect crust is getting the grill as hot as possible and using a two-zone setup. You'll want to grill the steak over direct heat, flipping it every 20 to 30 seconds as you cook it, while also moving it back and forth from the direct- and indirect-cooking zones. Don't be afraid to flip it and move it as much as you need to, to avoid burning the surface. If a steak is drier, like a dry-aged steak, it will sear more quickly than a fresh steak, so it should be flipped every 10 to 15 seconds.

Basting the steak with butter will also help it develop a nice crust, especially for steaks that don't have a lot of fat. As the butter caramelizes, it will give the steak a nice crust and also give it incredible flavor. Just be aware that if you baste over coals, there will be flare-ups. A little bit of flame kissing your steaks is okay, just as long as you don't let anything turn black. You also want to avoid trying to add a crust to a surface area that is not hot enough. If a steak isn't super hot before you begin basting it, the butter will boil the meat instead of creating that wonderful crust. The steak surface needs to be really hot before you begin basting!

Another helpful step is to pat the steak dry with paper towels before searing it. The enemy of a good sear is moisture.

CREATING GRILL MARKS

Grill marks on chicken and fish are actualy okay. It's difficult to get a golden-brown crust on chicken or fish because of the low fat content in the meat. I actually enjoy the flavor of grill marks on chicken and fish, but hate it on steaks and pork.

THE REVERSE-SEAR TECHNIQUE

A reverse sear is when you first cook the food on the indirect side, using the radiant heat to cook, and then add a sear at the end of the process. This method can give you more control over the cook and help ensure you don't overcook the food. This is a nice and gentle way to cook that takes a little longer than pure direct grilling, but it can yield better results.

THE "COLD" GRATE TECHNIQUE

The "cold" grate technique is when you build a fire on one side of the grill and then rotate the grill grate frequently to avoid the grate from getting so hot that it creates grill marks on the meat. Once the side that is over the flames gets nice and hot, you rotate the grate away from the flames so that the "cold" side is then over the flames. You continue this process until the steak is fully seared and has a nice golden-brown crust.

Grill marks

FREEZING MEAT

There is nothing wrong with freezing meat, just as long as it's done properly. I have eaten steaks that have been frozen for up to a year and they've still tasted great, but you need to make sure freezing is done properly to ensure the meat remains fresh, even after freezing.

The most important thing to prevent when freezing meat is freezer burn. Freezer burn is a discoloration of meat caused by a loss of moisture due to bad packaging. It can cause meat to become tough and dry.

VACUUM SEALERS AND VACUUM CHAMBERS

The best way to prepare meat for freezing is using a vacuum sealer. Vacuum sealers are relatively inexpensive and work by removing air from the bag that holds the meat. Investing in a vacuum sealer can actually save you money because you can buy meat in bulk, cut it yourself and to your liking, and then freeze it. The high-quality seal of the vacuum sealer will ensure the meat will last longer than if it's just wrapped. If money is not an issue, invest in a vacuum chamber. They're expensive, but they're what big meat companies use, and also what I use to seal meat. It allows me to break down large primal cuts and save big bucks.

Whether you use a vacuum sealer or a vacuum chamber, good preparation is key. Keep the bag, and the edges of the bag in particular, clean and free of liquids to ensure a perfect seal. It will give you a better finished product, and the meat will last a lot longer in the freezer.

OTHER METHODS

Simply wrapping meat for freezing is less than ideal. But if you do wrap meat for freezing, you need to remove as much of the air from the packaging as possible. You'll want to double wrap the cuts in plastic wrap or freezer paper, or seal them in freezer bags. If you use freezer bags, you can use the water displacement method to seal meat. Place the meat in a ziplock bag, leaving a very small opening to allow the air to escape. Submerge the bag in a large pot of cold water. (The air will be forced out of the bag as you submerge it.) Once fully submerged, seal the bag.

TENDERIZING METHODS

Some cuts of meat tend to dry out as they are being cooked. This mostly applies to large cuts of meat, like brisket or cuts used for pot roasts, due to the amount of connective tissue they have and the fact that they are not as tender as other cuts of meat. Here are some tricks you can use to tenderize meat and also keep it from drying out as it cooks.

STEAMING

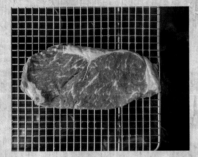

Steaming unwrapped meat can be an effective way to tenderize tougher cuts. It also allows you to infuse different flavors into the meat by steaming it with liquids like beer, wine, or even tea! Steaming can also be done in a smoker. Loosely wrapping cuts like brisket or short ribs in butcher paper during the smoking process allows some steam to escape, but still keeps enough steam around the meat to ensure the bark (the outer coating that comes from the smoking process) remains soft. Texas BBQ is known for its perfect bark, and anyone who's tried it knows this steaming process is why the bark is so good. Wrapping in butcher paper only lightly steams the meat, creating the perfect bark.

Wrapping brisket or short ribs in aluminum foil would make the bark too soft and soggy, but it can still work for other cuts. I use foil to steam meat quite often if I am in a hurry. Many people like to create a "boat" with the foil and leave the top area exposed, which will allow you to get the meat extremely tender and still have that Texas-style bark.

ENZYMES

Many countries use fruit to tenderize meat. Fruit contains an enzyme called *bromelain*, and it will literally cause meat to disintegrate if you let it sit for too long. You can use enzymes to tenderize meat by grinding the fruit into a paste and applying it to the surface of the meat. Don't let it sit long—30 minutes is plenty; any longer and your steak will be like ground beef. Avoid using processed enzymes. Instead, use fresh fruits like pineapple and papaya. Just be sure to wash off the paste once the desired tenderizing time has been achieved.

MECHANICAL

You can use almost anything for this method: a meat mallet works great; a jaccard is great. My aunt used to tenderize steaks with a cast-iron skillet; she would just hammer the meat until it was flat. Whatever tenderizing weapon you choose, keep two things in mind: it will change the shape of the meat, and you must be careful about how much you do it. The more you do it, the more tender the meat will be.

SEASONING METHODS

Seasoning is subjective. What works for some people doesn't necessarily work for others, and that's why I often don't include exact measurements for basic seasonings in my recipes. With that said, there are several different ways to season meat. And each way can change the flavors and textures, and result in different outcomes.

SALTING

Don't be afraid to use salt! Salt is your best friend when it comes to cooking amazing-tasting steaks and other cuts. If you've ever had a delicious steak at a restaurant and wondered why your steaks don't taste like that at home, it's probably because you didn't season the steak properly prior to cooking. Most people tend to underseason steaks, as well as large primal cuts like briskets and rib roasts.

The key to seasoning with salt is using coarse kosher salt. Coarse salt has a larger grain and allows you to have more control over the amount you add. It can be easy to overseason a steak with fine salt, which has a very fine grain and is more difficult to control.

When deciding how heavily to season with salt, a good rule of thumb is to cover the steak completely, but without covering it to the point where you can no longer see the meat. If you're unsure of how much salt to use, you can underseason the meat

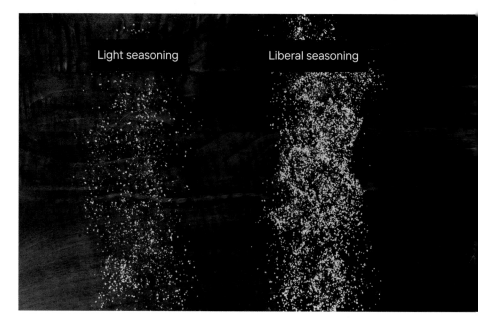

Light seasoning   Liberal seasoning

and add additional salt once the meat is fully cooked. I'm not a huge fan of this method, as the salt that is added after cooking will only be on the surface of the meat and it won't be as flavorful, but it's a better approach than overseasoning the meat before you cook. If you want to take the seasoning to the next level, there are finishing salts you can use on meat after it's fully cooked. These salts come in many flavors.

RUBS

Rubs are all very different in their own ways. Some rubs make meat sweet, some make it savory, and others make it spicy. Rubs like my own all-purpose rub don't change the flavor of the meat, but enhance it. That's important when choosing a rub. You want it to enhance the flavor of the meat without taking away from the flavor of the meat. The best way to know if a rub will be good on meat is to taste it. If it tastes good alone, it's probably going to taste good on a steak!

HERBS

Fresh and dried herbs can be used to season meats, both before cooking and during cooking. I like to create an herb brush by tying a sprig of fresh rosemary or thyme to a basting brush and then using the herb "brush" to baste a steak with melted butter. Be careful with some herbs; they can overpower the flavor of the meat. Season lightly and adjust as you become more familiar with the herb and how it affects the meat.

DRY BRINING

Dry brining sounds complicated, but it's really just the process of covering meat with salt and letting it penetrate and season the meat, usually overnight in the fridge. Unlike with seasoning, with dry brining you cover the entire surface of the cut with coarse kosher salt to the point where you can't see the meat. You then let it sit in the refrigerator, uncovered, for at least 4 hours, or even better, overnight. While the meat is brining, the salt will draw moisture out of the meat and create a nice salty solution on the surface of the meat. The steak will then reabsorb the salty solution and ensure that the steak is fully seasoned all the way through, and not just on the surface.

DRY AGING

Dry aging is a method of preserving meat by keeping it in a cold, dry location over an extended period of time. This process causes the exterior of the meat to dry out, but preserves the inside of the meat and gives it a very unique flavor. Dry aging works by keeping meat at a certain temperature and humidity level, causing the water from the exterior of the meat to evaporate, which then dries out the exterior and creates a protective outer coating known as *pellicles*. The pellicles protect the interior of the meat and prevent it from spoiling. This process actually tenderizes the meat and gives it additional flavor described by some as a "funk" that is similar to an aged wine or an aged cheese.

The easiest way to dry age meat at home is in a dry aging cabinet. A dry aging cabinet controls everything, so you just set the meat inside the cabinet and let it dry age for as long as you like. While these cabinets are great to have, they're also somewhat expensive. A less expensive way to dry age meat is to place it in a special bag that is made specifically for dry aging. A dry aging bag allows moisture to escape from the meat, while still allowing the protective pellicles to form on the surface of the meat. To dry age meat in a dry aging bag, place the meat in the bag and then place the bag on a cooling rack. Place the bag and cooling rack in the fridge and let it dry age for as long as you like. Once the meat has aged, remove it from the bag and then use a butcher's knife to remove the pellicles from the exterior of the steaks before seasoning and cooking.

COOKING TEMPERATURES

Cooking temperatures are subjective. What I prefer for a final temperature is not necessarily what others will prefer, but these temperatures are what I go by. And while this guide is what I believe is the best and most reasonable, it's up to you to decide what is best for you. Also, keep in mind that these are the final temperatures after resting times. While resting, the temperature of meat can rise anywhere from 3 to 10 degrees, so you'll want to remove the meat from the heat before it reaches the final cooking temperature.

BEEF

Ribeye: 135°F (57°C)

Filet mignon: 125°F (52°C)

New York strip: 130°F (54°C)

Chateaubriand: 125°F (52°C)

Tenderloin roast: 120°F (49°C)

Striploin roast: 135°F (57°C)

Picanha (top sirloin cap): 135°F (57°C)

Prime rib: 135°F (57°C)

Short rib: 200°F (93°C)

Skirt steak: 140°F (60°C)

Flat iron steak: 135°F (57°C)

Tri tip: 135°F (57°C)

Porterhouse: 130°F (54°C)

T-bone: 130°F (54°C)

Sirloin: 120°F (49°C)

Hanger steak: 135°F (57°C)

Flank steak: 135°F (57°C)

Brisket: 205°F (96°C)

Beef ribs: 200°F (93°C)

Beef cheeks: 200°F (93°C)

Beef tongue: 190°F (88°C)

PORK

Pork butt: 205°F (96°C)

Pork belly: 180°F (82°C)

Pork chop: 145°F (63°C)

Pork tenderloin: 145°F (63°C)

Pork shoulder: 205°F (96°C)

Pork ribs: 190°F–200°F (88°C– 93°C)

Iberico Secreto : 145°F (63°C)

POULTRY

Chicken breast: 165°F (74°C)

Chicken thighs: 175°F (79°C)

Chicken wings: 175°F (79°C)

Turkey thighs: 175°F (79°C)

Turkey breast: 165°F (74°C)

OTHER MEATS

Rack of lamb: 135°F (57°C)

Rabbit: 165°F (74°C)

RESTING TIMES

Meat releases juices as it is being cooked because heat causes the muscle fibers to contract, which pushes the juices out of the meat. By letting meat rest after cooking, you give the muscle fibers time to relax and reabsorb the juices. How long you let cooked meats rest after cooking will vary depending on the type of meat and the cut.

BEEF

Steak: rested 3 to 7 minutes.

Brisket: wrapped in butcher paper and rested 1 to 12 hours in a food warmer or oven, set at 150°F (66°C).

Beef ribs: wrapped in butcher paper and rested 1 to 12 hours in a food warmer or oven, set at 150°F (66°C).

Prime rib: wrapped in aluminum foil and rested 20 minutes to 1 hour in a cold oven.

Tenderloin roast: wrapped in aluminum foil and rested 10 to 30 minutes in a cold oven.

Striploin roast: wrapped in aluminum foil and rested 20 minutes to 1 hour in a cold oven.

PORK

Pork shoulder: wrapped in aluminum foil and rested 1 to 7 hours in a food warmer or oven, set at 150°F (66°C).

Pork ribs: wrapped in butcher paper and rested 30 minutes to 4 hours in a food warmer or oven set at 150°F (66°C).

Pork butt: rested 1 to 7 hours in a food warmer or oven, set at 150°F (66°C).

Pork belly: wrapped in aluminum foil and rested 30 to 45 minutes in a cold oven.

Pork loin: loosely covered with aluminum foil and rested 5 to 10 minutes.

POULTRY AND LAMB

Chicken: loosely covered with aluminum foil and rested 2 to 5 minutes.

Turkey breast: loosely covered with aluminum foil and rested 5 to 10 minutes.

Rack of lamb: loosely covered with aluminum foil and rested 5 to 15 minutes.

DO IT LIKE GUGA!

There is a trade-off with letting meat rest: it will not be as hot as it would be if you were to cut into it right away. But cutting into meat right away also means you're likely to lose a lot of the juices. (Growing up in the countryside in Brazil, I don't recall us ever letting meat rest before we sliced it; we just dug in!) The point of letting meat rest is to let the fibers relax a bit and to help them retain more juice, but if you want to dive in right away, that's okay; just don't discard the juices. Do I, Guga, let meat rest every time I cook? Heck no! Sometimes I cut straight into it, but I always make sure to reserve the juices on the cutting board so I can dip the meat into those amazing juices. (I like to serve rice on the plate and cut my steaks next to the rice so no juices go to waste!) In the end, the decision is yours. If you're really hungry and want your meat hot, just slice it and eat it right away. If you prefer to let it rest, go for it. Either way, just remember to save me a piece!

BEEF

BEEF

I was born in Uberaba, Minas Gerais, Brazil. Uberaba is known as the big cattle city in Brazil. It's where most of the auctions of extremely expensive cows take place. This city is where my passion for beef started. And if you know me, you know I love beef!

This type of meat has been hunted and eaten for thousands of years and is one of the most common kinds of meat found today. There are several different breeds of cattle that result in different kinds of beef. In this section, you'll learn about different cattle breeds and the most common cuts of beef. You'll also learn what makes good beef and what to look for when buying it.

THE CUTS

Different countries have different names for beef cuts, but in the end, beef is beef, and that is all that matters because it is all really delicious! However, every cut should be treated differently as you cook it.

Japanese Wagyu A5 filet mignon

FOREQUARTER CUTS

Forequarter cuts are usually tough and should be treated with more attention to detail.

Brisket Brisket comes from the lower chest area of the cow. When it's cooked properly, a brisket is absolutely amazing, but it can be perfect or a disaster because every brisket is a little different.

Chuck Chuck is one of the cheaper cuts of meat due to its toughness. This cut can be delicious and tender if you take your time when you cook it. If it's done right, it can even be more delicious than expensive cuts.

Foreshank Foreshank is great to use for soups or stocks due to the high collagen in the meat. It's also used to make flavorful consommés because the meat has such a rich flavor.

Plate Beef plate is where short ribs, skirt steak, and hanger steak come from. Skirt steak is usually marinated and seared over high heat. Higher quality skirt steak should not be marinated because you want to be able to taste the meat. This is a delicious steak that can have several different flavors depending how you season it.

Short ribs Short ribs are hands down my favorite cut of beef after the queen: picanha. It should be cooked slowly over time so the fat can render down to collagen, which is extremely flavorful and what I crave the most.

Rib The rib produces some of the most popular cuts of beef, including ribeye and prime rib roast.

HINDQUARTER CUTS

Hindquarter cuts are more tender and require a little less effort to cook than forequarter cuts, but they still require a watchful eye on the grill.

Flank Flank steak gets a bad rap because it's not a popular cut like ribeye or New York strip, but if it's cooked properly, it can be even better. I like to cook this cut between medium rare and medium because of the way the fat renders at that temperature. I think it results in better flavor.

Round The round is one of the most undesirable cuts of the cow. That's why it's so cheap! The flavor is great, but it's very tough, so it's mostly used for roasts. I've been trying for years to make round as tender as a steak, but I've still not prevailed. (But I will one day! Mark my words!)

Sirloin The sirloin is home to the tri tip and, obviously, the sirloin steak. Sirloin is split into two parts: top sirloin and bottom sirloin. The top sirloin is where the sirloin steak comes from and is great for grilling. The bottom sirloin is where the tri tip comes from, and that cut is usually used for roasting and slow cooks.

Loin The loin is where the tenderloin, New York strip, and filet mignon come from. (Filet Mignon is my nephew, Angel's, favorite because it's the most tender cut of beef.) Filet mignon might be expensive and a smaller cut, but it sure packs a lot of flavor and is worth every penny! New York strip is an excellent and flavorful cut.

WHAT MAKES GOOD BEEF?

What make beef taste so amazing is the fat content in the meat, but there are other factors that have a big impact as well.

Marbling Marbling is the fat content in the meat. When you look at a steak and you see the white specks and streaks throughout the meat, that is the marbling. Marbling is not the fat on the outside of the meat. The more marbling a steak has, the better it is. Remember: fat is flavor!

Tenderness Muscles that work less in the cow are more tender and have a higher fat content. That's why they are so desirable and also so expensive. Steaks like filet mignon, ribeye, and New York strip are the most popular because of their tenderness and incredible flavor. They can be a bit expensive, but for good reason! If you want a really tender steak, avoid cuts from working muscles.

Breeding There are big differences in breeding when it comes to meat. For example, Angus, Hereford, Texas longhorn, and Wagyu are some of the most popular cattle breeds. Angus is the more popular breed in the United States, while in Brazil, the most popular breed is Nelore. Each breed has a unique flavor profile.

Diet Diet affects the marbling and even the flavor of the meat. Wagyu cattle are typically fed high-energy ingredients like hay, grain, and wheat. Olive Wagyu cattle are fed green olive pulp, which causes their meat to have a distinct taste and color.

HOW TO BUY BEEF

While many of the recipes in this book use the best of the best, it's important to know that you can use whatever grade of beef you want for any of the recipes. I just like to use the very best; it means I'm getting the full experience. With that said, I encourage you to simply buy the best quality you can afford. Many supermarkets have great selections of beef, but a local meat dealer or butcher might have a little more variety and a little higher quality, but also they may be more expensive. Whatever you can afford is exactly what you should use.

USDA GRADING

When you shop for beef, the packaging will include a quality grade. Here are the common grades you'll find in the United States.

Prime Prime beef comes from young, well-fed cattle. It is the highest grading scale available in the United States. It's the best meat you can buy because of the excellent marbling in the meat. It will be the most flavorful of any of the grades.

Choice Choice is a grade below prime beef, but is easily accessible in every grocery store, whereas prime may be a bit more difficult to find. Choice is still good beef with a bit less marbling in the meat than prime, but it will still be delicious.

Select Select is the lowest quality beef you can buy, and I highly recommend avoiding it. It is typically very lean and doesn't have a lot of marbling in the meat. This grade is usually cheap and the price speaks for itself.

COMMON BEEF BREEDS

In addition to the grading, some beef may include the breed on the packaging. The breed can have a big impact on flavor. These are the most common breeds you'll find in the United States.

Angus Angus is a breed of cattle that was discovered in Scotland in the mid 19th century. It's best known for its marbling, consistency, and juicy flavor. It has become one of the most popular breeds you can buy in the United States.

Hereford Hereford is a British breed of beef, originally from Herefordshire in England. It's not as popular in the United States as Angus beef, but it is still good and is known for the well-marbled and flavorful meat that it provides.

WAGYU BEEF BREEDS

In addition to the common breeds, there are some premium breeds that take flavor to an entirely new level. The meat from some of these breeds is used in several recipes in this book, and while the meat from these breeds is more expensive than what you'll find in the grocery store, it's absolutely amazing and worth the money, if you can afford it. Wagyu beef is usually bred in Japan, Australia, and the United States. It has several different gradings based on the marbling in the meat.

Japanese and Australian Wagyu Japanese Wagyu has a grading scale from A1 to A5, with A5 being the most expensive and sought-after meat in the world due to the insane marbling in the meat. This marbling is due to a grain-only diet they're fed, which results in larger and fattier cattle. This meat is considered the best in the world. It's so rich that it's virtually impossible to eat an entire steak by yourself due to the amount of fat in the meat. Because of this, it's usually paired with a side dish or something else to help cut the richness from the fat. Australian Wagyu is also very high quality, but it's less fatty than Japanese Wagyu, so you can enjoy an entire steak without it becoming too overbearing.

American Wagyu American Wagyu is better than the prime beef you'll find in most stores, but it's not as good as Japanese or Australian Wagyu. With that said, this amazing meat is easier to access in the United States than Japanese and Australian Wagyu. It's also a bit less expensive because it's not being imported. If you don't have easy access to a meat dealer who can get you Japanese or Australian Wagyu, give American Wagyu a try. You won't be disappointed!

Kobe Kobe beef is Wagyu from the Tajima strain of Japanese Black cattle. The meat is considered a delicacy because of its wonderful flavor and tenderness. The cattle are only raised in a specific region of Japan due to rules established by the Kobe Beef Marketing and Distribution Promotion Association. Kobe beef must have a MS (marbling score) above 6. The marbling score is a grade given to meat based on the visible amount of intramuscular fat in the meat. This scale ranges from 3 to 12, with 12 being the highest grade. Kobe is usually prepared as steak, shabu-shabu, sashimi, and teppanyaki.

Olive Olive Wagyu comes from a type of cattle bred on the Japanese island of Shōdoshima. They get the name because of their diet, which consists of dried and roasted olives. This diet gives the meat a unique flavor and a softer fat. Olive Wagyu is graded as a Wagyu A5. The reason the meat is so rare is that there are very few olive Wagyu cows in the world. The exact numbers fluctuate, but I would estimate there are only a few thousand olive Wagyu cows in the world, with very few of them being harvested each month.

Hanwoo Hanwoo is a form of Wagyu, but it's raised in Korea. This cattle is fed mainly rice straw. This meat is a little more difficult to get than other Wagyu varieties because it is unavailable in the United States.

Australian Wagyu
MS7 New York strip

BEEF

THE RECIPES

SMOKED BRISKET

Oh yes, the brisket! You can officially graduate from "Backyard Pitmaster University" once you've finally achieved the perfect brisket. Traditional brisket takes anywhere from 8 to 12 hours to cook, depending on the size of the brisket and how done you want the final product to be. An internal temperature of 205°F (96°C) is most commonly considered done, but you should never rely solely on temperature to determine doneness. The doneness in smoked meats is measured by feel, not just by temperature. When you poke it with a toothpick and it feels like a warm knife moving through room-temperature butter, that's when you'll know it's done.

½ cup water

½ cup beef stock

½ cup apple cider vinegar

Coarse kosher salt

Ground black pepper

Yellow mustard or Worcestershire sauce

10–15lb (4.5–6.75kg) beef brisket, trimmed

Wagyu tallow or avocado oil (for coating the butcher paper)

PREP AND SEASONING

1   Combine the water, beef stock, and vinegar in a spray bottle. In a small bowl, combine equal amounts of the kosher salt and black pepper. Set aside.

2   Rub a very small amount of yellow mustard or Worcestershire sauce over the entire brisket. (This will serve as a binder so the seasonings will stick to the meat.)

3   Season the entire brisket liberally with the kosher salt and black pepper mixture.

LET'S DO IT!

1   Preheat the smoker to 250°F to 275°F (121°C to 135°C).

2   Place the brisket in the smoker. Smoke for 4 hours, spraying the brisket every 30 to 45 minutes with the vinegar–beef stock mixture to prevent a hard, crunchy crust from forming.

3   After 4 hours, check the brisket. If the color is to your liking, transfer the brisket to a large sheet of butcher paper that has been brushed with Wagyu tallow or avocado oil until it's moist, but not overly wet. Wrap the brisket tightly in the butcher paper.

4   Place the wrapped brisket back in the smoker. Continue smoking for an additional 4 to 8 hours or until the internal temperature reaches 200°F to 205°F (93°C to 96°C) and there is very little resistance when you poke the brisket through the butcher paper with a toothpick.

5   Remove the brisket from the smoker, and set it aside to rest for at least 1 hour or up to 12 hours (the longer, the better.) Place the brisket in a large cooler or an oven set to 150°F (66°C) to help keep it warm.

6   Remove the butcher paper and slice the rested brisket against the grain and into ¼-inch (0.65cm) pieces. Serve warm.

DO IT LIKE GUGA!

There is no absolute right or wrong color for the outer coating on the brisket (often referred to as the "bark"). Texas-style bark is usually closer to black, but some people don't like it that dark, so you should be the judge of what color looks right for you. I like mine in the midrange of color—not too dark but not too light, and more like a mahogany color.

TRIMMING BRISKET

A brisket is a big piece of meat and it can get pretty pricey, so you want to make sure you get the most out of it. For this reason, before cooking a brisket you'll want to trim any unnecessary or unusable meat or fat to make the brisket more uniformly shaped, which will help it cook more evenly. You don't want to have burnt crispy pieces or too much fat that isn't rendered and is inedible; you want the perfect fat-to-meat ratio that will result in a brisket that is tender and juicy.

Here are some tips for trimming brisket that will help you get perfect results every time:

- Use a sharp knife to remove any silver skin, excess fat, or loose flaps of meat on the meat side of the brisket. You want the meat side to be nice and smooth because this is the side that will be laying on the smoker or grill grate, so you want it to be nice and flat.

- The fattier, pointed end of the brisket is known as *the point,* while the leaner, flatter end of the brisket is known as *the flat.* Where the fatty side meets the lean muscle on the point, there will be a big chunk of fat you'll want to remove because it won't render as you're cooking the brisket.

- As you trim, you'll only want to leave about ¼ inch (.65cm) of fat on the meat. This will be the perfect amount and will allow the fat to render down nicely when cooking, resulting in a juicy brisket. (For a brisket that is prime grade or higher, you'll want to trim more of the fat from the point. For a leaner brisket, you'll want to trim less of the fat from the point. For the flat, always use ¼ inch [0.65cm] of fat as a good guide.)

- Once you've trimmed the fat, you'll want to give the brisket a nice shape. There is a big chunk of meat on the point with no fat; just make sure to round that piece off so there are no hard edges.

- You'll want to round out the sides of the brisket by removing any overhanging fat and meat and taking off any large chunks of fat or meat that will prevent the brisket from being nice and smooth. You don't want any sharp edges as those will burn and get extra crispy.

- Lastly, do not throw away the trimmings! Keep them for grinding into burgers or sausages.

Meat side

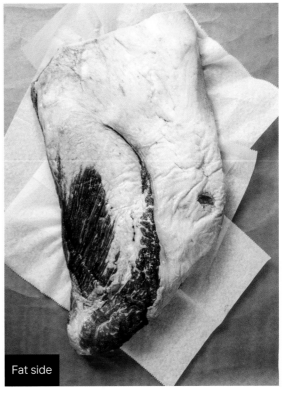

Fat side

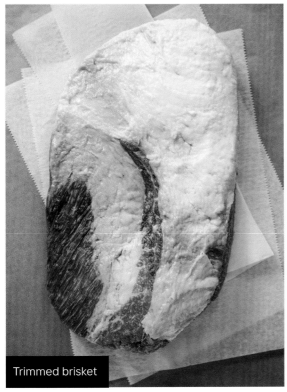

Trimmed brisket

Leave ¼ inch (0.65cm) of fat

DORITOS STEAK

It's time to get a bit crazy and try something different! This recipe uses Doritos as a crust and it's absolutely delicious. (I've also tried this recipe with Takis and Ruffles, and it's also turned out amazing.) Hopefully, this recipe will open your imagination and encourage you to try new things and discover new flavors. Pair this with Japanese Potato Salad (p. 188) for an incredible meal!

3 (8oz/225g) New York strip steaks

Coarse kosher salt

Ground black pepper

Garlic powder

1 (14.5oz/411g) bag Nacho Cheese Flavored Doritos

3 large eggs

1 cup all-purpose flour

4 cups avocado oil or Wagyu beef tallow

FOR THE SAUCE

3 tbsp sour cream

1 tbsp Greek Yogurt Horseradish Sauce (p. 205)

2 tbsp mayonnaise

1 tsp sherry vinegar

1 tsp Worcestershire sauce

1 tbsp Doritos® Dust (p. 215)

Coarse kosher salt, to taste

PREP AND SEASONING

1   Season the steaks liberally with kosher salt, black pepper, and garlic powder. Set aside.

2   Working in batches, process the Doritos® in a food processor until they form a fine powder. Set aside.

3   Make the sauce by combining the sour cream, Greek Yogurt Horseradish Sauce, mayonnaise, sherry vinegar, Worcestershire sauce, and Doritos® Dust in a small bowl. Season to taste with kosher salt, stir, and then cover with plastic wrap. Place in the fridge until ready to serve.

4   Whisk the eggs in a shallow dish. Set aside.

5   Add the all-purpose flour and processed Doritos® to separate shallow dishes. Set aside.

LET'S DO IT!

1   Set up the grill for two-zone cooking. Preheat to 250°F (121°C).

2   Place the steaks over indirect heat. Cook for 30 to 45 minutes or until the steaks reach an internal temperature of 130°F (54°C).

3   Once the steaks reach the correct temperature, remove them from the grill and dredge them in the flour. Shake gently to remove any excess, and then dip them into the egg wash followed by the powdered Doritos®. Set aside.

4   Add the avocado oil to a large cast-iron skillet over medium-high heat. Heat the oil to 400°F (204°C).

5   Once the oil reaches the proper temperature, carefully flash fry the steaks in the oil for 1 to 2 minutes each, flipping them continuously, until they develop a nice crust. (The powder that imparts red color to the Doritos® will dissipate into the oil, so the crust will actually become lighter as you fry the steaks. If you overcook the steaks, the crust will turn dark and will taste bitter.)

6   Transfer the steaks to a cutting board. Allow to rest for 5 to 10 minutes before slicing thinly. Serve with the sauce on the side. (The steaks will be juicy on the inside, but the crust will be a little dry because you flash fried the steaks. The sauce will help with the dryness and also give the steaks a wonderful flavor!)

DO IT LIKE GUGA!

I used to use New York strip steaks for this recipe, but you can use any thick cut of steak you like. Ribeye or filet mignon would both work well; you'll just want to make sure the steaks are at least 1½ to 2 inches (3.75 to 5cm) thick. A beef roast would also work with this recipe. Thin-cut steaks like skirt steak won't work as well.

GRILLED PICANHA

In Brazil, picanha is called *Rainha das Carnes,* which translates to "Queen of All Meats." It's earned this name because of its incredible flavor and tenderness; most people describe it as a combination of the tenderness of filet mignon with the flavor of ribeye steak. This is the best piece of meat in the world and my favorite. It's as good as it gets!

3–5lb (1.35–2.25kg) picanha (top sirloin cap)

Coarse kosher salt

PREP AND SEASONING

1   Pat the picanha dry with paper towels.

2   Using a boning knife, remove all of the silver skin from only the meat side of the picanha.

3   Flip the picanha over and use the knife to remove any additional fat, if necessary. (You don't want to remove all the fat from the picanha; you want to leave about ¼ inch [0.65cm] around the entire piece.)

4   Locate the direction of the grain. Cutting with the grain, slice the picanha into five or six 1- to 1½-inch-thick (2.5- to 3.8cm-thick) steaks. (I prefer 1½-inch-thick steaks, which allow a strong sear on the steaks without overcooking them.)

5   Liberally season the steaks with coarse kosher salt, making sure to also season the fat. (To keep it traditional, you'll only want to use coarse kosher salt to season the picanha.)

TIP *For an even more tender result and deeper seasoning, try dry brining the picanha overnight prior to grilling.*

LET'S DO IT!

1   Set up the grill for two-zone cooking. Preheat to 250°F (121°C).

2   Place the steaks on the grill over indirect heat. Cook for approximately 20 minutes, flipping them frequently, until the internal temperature reaches 125°F (52°C).

3   Move the steaks directly over the coals and sear until golden brown. (Keep moving and flipping the steaks until you get the perfect sear. If flare-ups occur, don't let the flames kiss the steaks for any longer than a few seconds.)

4   Transfer the steaks to a cutting board to rest for 5 to 10 minutes.

5   Cut the rested steaks against the grain and into thin slices.

6   Collect the juices from the cutting board, and drizzle them over the top of the sliced picanha. Serve warm.

DO IT LIKE GUGA!

Picanha has lots of fat. The key to grilling it properly is to get a golden-brown color on the steak and a dark golden-brown color on the fat, but without burning the fat. You don't want grill marks or a char on the meat or the fat!

SMOKED PICANHA

Forget about using only salt for this one! For smoking picanha, you'll want to season the meat with your favorite rub, or you can use one of my rubs. This is a thick piece of meat, so seasoning it properly is crucial to getting a great-tasting smoked picanha.

3–5lb (1.35–2.25kg) picanha (top sirloin cap)

Coarse kosher salt

Guga's BBQ Rub (p. 200) or other BBQ rub of your choice

PREP AND SEASONING

1   Pat the picanha dry with paper towels.

2   Using a boning knife, remove the silver skin from only the meat side of the picanha.

3   Flip the picanha over to expose the fat side. Score the fat cap and underlying silver skin in a criss-cross pattern to about the same width you will be cutting your slices, but try not to cut too far into the meat. I like to cut my slices to about ¼ inch wide (0.65cm). (If the fat cap and the underlying silver skin aren't scored, the end of the picanha will curl into a ball.)

4   Lightly season all sides with kosher salt, and then liberally season all sides with Guga's BBQ Rub.

LET'S DO IT!

1   Preheat the smoker to 250°F (121°C). (This temperature will yield a medium-rare to medium result, with the edges being be more medium. If you prefer a fully medium-rare result, reduce the smoker temperature to 200°F [93°C].)

2   Place the picanha in the smoker. Cook until the internal temperature reaches 135°F (57°C), about 1 hour.

3   While the picanha is smoking, set up the grill for direct cooking and preheat to 500°F (260°C). (Make sure the fire is hot!)

4   When the picanha reaches the proper temperature, remove it from the smoker and pat it dry with paper towels.

5   Using long tongs, hold the picanha on the hot grill surface. Sear the meat sides first, and then sear the fat cap. Expect fire, *lots* of fire. Remember that fat burns quickly, but you don't want to burn the fat. You are looking for golden-brown color. (If you don't have a grill, move the meat to the rack closest to the fire box in the smoker to get the sear. If you are already using your grill to smoke the picanha, you'll need to make sure you set up your grill for two-zone cooking.)

6   Immediately wrap the picanha tightly in aluminum foil. Set it aside to rest for at least 10 minutes.

7   Slice the rested picanha against the grain and into ¼-inch-wide (0.65cm-wide) slices. (Congratulations! Heaven has just opened up!)

CRUNCHY BARK OR SOFT BARK?

If you like your bark crunchier, there is no need to do anything special to the ribs. Just smoke them! But if you like a nice soft bark, which is what I recommend, you'll want to keep the ribs as moist as possible. You can achieve this by spraying the ribs every 30 minutes with just water or a seasoned liquid using 3 parts water and 1 part seasoning liquid. Here are a few seasoning liquid options:

- Apple cider vinegar (for a more acidic flavor)
- Apple juice (for a sweeter flavor)
- Worcestershire sauce (for a beefier flavor)
- Beef stock (will not modify flavor)
- Coca-Cola (for a sweeter flavor and a darker bark)
- Lime juice (for a Latin flavor)

TEXAS-STYLE SMOKED SHORT RIBS

After picanha, short ribs are my favorite cut of meat; they're versatile and can be barbecued, grilled, smoked, pressure cooked, and even panfried. And each method will yield different results and textures. I recommend serving these amazing ribs with Roasted Garlic Mashed Potatoes (p. 176), Pickled Red Onions (p. 187), Pickled Korean Cucumbers (p. 184), and Garlic Bread (p. 185).

5–10lb (2.25–4.5kg) short ribs

1 cup coarse kosher salt

1 cup ground black pepper

Guga's BBQ Rub (p. 200)

TIP *When you open a package of short ribs, they can have a strong, beefy smell, which can be stronger than any other cut of beef. This smell is because of the bones, but don't be alarmed, this is normal.*

PREP AND SEASONING

1 Make the rub by combining the kosher salt and black pepper in a medium bowl. Set aside.

2 Pat the ribs dry with paper towels. (If needed, dampen the paper towels to remove as much of the meat juices as possible from the bones.)

3 Remove most of the external top fat to expose the meat. (This will allow the salt to better penetrate the meat.)

4 Use a sharp knife to remove the silver skin. (Don't remove the silver skin on the bones, which can compromise the structure of the short ribs when smoking. After the silver skin on the bones is cooked, it will be like a crispy, crunchy chicharron that can be eaten!)

5 Liberally season the ribs with the salt and pepper mix and then lightly season with Guga's BBQ Rub.

LET'S DO IT!

1 Preheat the smoker to 275°F (135°C). Once the smoker reaches temperature, wait 20 minutes before adding the short ribs.

2 Place the short ribs in the smoker and as far away from the heat source as possible. (The goal is to get smoke flavor on the ribs, but not to cook them completely.)

3 Smoke for 4 hours or until you are happy with the color. (I look for a dark golden-brown color. The more golden the color, the more flavorful the ribs. The color will vary from smoker to smoker and will depend on how you are running your fire.)

4 After 4 hours, wrap the ribs to finish the cook. (For a faster cook [1 to 3 hours] and an extremely soft bark, wrap the ribs in aluminum foil, being extra careful not to damage the bark. For a dryer bark and a longer cook [2 to 5 hours], wrap the ribs in butcher paper.) Place the wrapped ribs back in the smoker.)

5 After 1 to 2 hours, poke the meat with a toothpick. If it feels like a knife going through room-temperature butter, use a meat thermometer to check the temperature. If the temperature is 200°F to 205°F (93°C to 96°C), the ribs are done. If the ribs are not at temperature, place them back in the smoker and check them every 45 minutes to 1 hour until they are done.

6 Remove the ribs from the smoker. Set aside to rest in a closed container like a cold oven or cooler for a minimum of 1 hour and up to 12 hours. (If you need to let the ribs rest for longer than 4 hours, set your oven to the lowest setting and place the fully wrapped ribs in the oven for up to 12 hours.)

7 Slice into individual ribs. Serve warm. (Always serve with the bones. One of the most amazing parts of the short ribs is the crispy skin that is left on the bones.)

ROASTED GARLIC RIBEYE

While picanha is "Queen of All Meats," many say ribeye steak is king! I somewhat agree because ribeye provides the best bite on the cow—I am talking about the *spinalis dorsi,* also known as the ribeye cap. When I was young, I would eat all the steak but save the cap as my last bite. Man, is it good! It's amazing! Here is one of the best ways to make it.

2 (1lb/454g) ribeye steaks, each about 1½ inches (3.75cm) thick

Coarse kosher salt

Ground black pepper

Granulated garlic

5 sprigs fresh thyme, divided

1 tbsp grapeseed or avocado oil

4 tbsp unsalted butter

8 garlic cloves

FOR THE ROASTED GARLIC COMPOUND BUTTER

2 large garlic heads

Olive oil

Coarse kosher salt

Ground black pepper

8 tbsp unsalted butter, softened

1 tsp dried parsley

PREP AND SEASONING

1   Preheat the oven to 375°F (190°C).

2   Pat the steaks dry with paper towels. Liberally season all sides with kosher salt, black pepper, and granulated garlic. Tightly wrap the steaks in plastic wrap and transfer to the fridge to rest.

3   Begin making the compound butter by slicing the tops from the garlic heads to expose a small portion of the cloves. Drizzle olive oil over the top of the heads and then season with kosher salt and black pepper.

4   Loosely wrap the trimmed garlic heads in aluminum foil. Bake for 40 minutes to 1 hour, checking the heads every 10 minutes to ensure they aren't burning. When the heads have a nice golden-brown color, remove them from the oven.

5   Carefully squeeze the heads to expel the cloves out onto a plate. Mash with a fork until a paste is formed. Allow to cool for 10 minutes.

6   Using the fork, combine the softened butter with the garlic paste and then add the dried parsley. Mash again until well combined. Place the butter on a sheet of plastic wrap. Mold the butter into a log and then transfer it to the fridge to set.

LET'S DO IT!

1   Set up the grill for two-zone cooking. Preheat to 250°F (121°C). Remove the steaks from the fridge.

2   Tie two thyme sprigs together with butcher's twine. Repeat with two more sprigs. Place the steaks over indirect heat, and then place the thyme sprigs on top of the steaks.

3   Grill for 20 minutes, turning the steaks occasionally, while moving the thyme sprigs to the top sides of the steaks, until the internal temperature reaches 120°F (49°C).

4   Preheat a cast-iron skillet over direct heat. When the skillet begins to smoke, add the grapeseed oil.

5   Place the steaks in the hot skillet and sear for 1 minute per side. Flip the steaks once more, and then move the skillet over to the indirect heat. Add the butter, remaining thyme sprig, and garlic cloves to the hot skillet. (If you have too much rendered fat after the first sear, remove the steaks and clean the skillet before adding the butter, thyme, and garlic.)

6   Wearing heat protective gloves, tilt the pan and then use a large spoon to baste the steaks in the butter continuously for 1 minute per side or until golden brown. (Be careful not to burn the butter! It's ok to have brown butter, but not black [burnt] butter.)

7   Transfer the steaks from the skillet to a cutting board to rest for 5 to 10 minutes. Top each steak with 1 tablespoon of the roasted garlic compound butter.

8   Use a knife to separate the eye from the cap and then remove any silver skin from cap. Slice the eye and cap into ½-inch (1.25cm) slices and serve.

DO IT LIKE GUGA!

Don't throw away the garlic cloves when you're done cooking! Instead, wrap a clove in a slice of ribeye and then take a bite of this amazingly sweet, savory, and delicious garlic steak!

CRAZY-DELICIOUS SKIRT STEAK

Whichever restaurant you go to in Miami, there's a good chance they will have skirt steak on the menu. And most restaurants charge a high price for this steak, and for good reason—it's amazing! It's also my wife's favorite steak (after "Queen of All Meats," of course).

3 medium skirt steaks (about 2lb/905g total)

Coarse kosher salt

Ground black pepper

Granulated garlic

FOR THE BASTING BUTTER

4 tbsp unsalted butter, melted

1 tbsp garlic paste

1 tsp dried parsley

2 tbsp Worcestershire sauce

PREP AND SEASONING

1 Pat the steaks dry with paper towels. (If the steaks have a lot of external fat, you can trim them a bit, but I recommend not trimming off too much. Fat is flavor, baby!)

2 Season the steaks liberally with kosher salt, black pepper, and granulated garlic. Set aside.

3 In a small bowl, use a fork to mash together the melted butter, garlic paste, dried parsley, and Worcestershire sauce. (Get your basting brush ready!)

TIP *You can use inside skirt, outside skirt, and even flap meat for this recipe, but outside skirt is the best choice. You can also cook this steak in a cast-iron or carbon steel pan—both will work great. Avoid cooking in a nonstick pan. You want to cook it fast and hot, and a nonstick pan will not get as hot as cast-iron or carbon steel pans.*

LET'S DO IT!

1 Set up your grill for two-zone cooking. Preheat to 400°F (204°C).

2 Grill the steaks over direct heat for 1 minute 30 seconds per side and then move them to indirect heat. Baste both sides with that amazing basting butter.

3 Now get ready! Using long tongs, move the steaks back to direct heat for 30 seconds per side. (There are going to be flare-ups as the butter melts into the fire, but that is what you want! When the butter hits the flames, it will vaporize and the flavor vapors will go back up onto the steaks. Just be sure not to leave the steaks over direct heat for more than 30 seconds per side. Otherwise, they could develop a bitter flavor.)

4 Move the steaks back to indirect heat, and check the internal temperature. You are looking for a final internal temperature of 135°F to 140°F (57°C to 60°C). If the temperature is too low, keep the steaks over the indirect heat until you achieve the desired temperature.

5 Once the steaks reach the desired temperature, set them aside to rest for 5 to 10 minutes before serving.

DO IT LIKE GUGA!

When I cook these steaks, I baste them directly over the charcoal, which can cause flare-ups. If you see a flare-up, don't move the steaks right away. Instead, wait 10 to 15 seconds and then move the steaks away from the flames. Try this and you'll notice that the steaks that are kissed by the flare-ups actually taste better than those that are not!

GALBI KOREAN GRILLED SHORT RIBS

One of my favorite memories from my childhood was the time I spent with a Korean taekwondo master who often took me to amazing Korean restaurants. This delicious recipe reminds me of those times.

8lb (3.5kg) flanken-style short ribs

FOR THE MARINADE

2 Asian pears, cored and chopped (you can use other varieties if you can't find Asian pears)

½ white sweet onion, diced

6 garlic cloves

½ tbsp minced ginger root

½ green onion, chopped

3 tbsp soy sauce

3 tbsp light brown sugar

2 tbsp honey

1½ tbsp coarse kosher salt

1 tbsp ground black pepper

1 tbsp sesame oil

PREP AND SEASONING

1 Pat the short ribs dry with paper towels. Set aside.

2 Make the marinade by combining the ingredients in a blender. Blend until smooth. (If needed, add water in small amounts until a marinade-like consistency is achieved.)

3 Place the short ribs in a large vacuum or freezer bag. Add the marinade, seal, and then rotate the bag gently to coat the ribs in the marinade.

4 Transfer the ribs to the fridge to marinate for at least 24 hours and up to 72 hours, rotating the bag every 12 hours to recoat the ribs in the marinade.

TIP *Flanken-style short ribs are cut thin and across the rib bones, as opposed to being cut between the rib bones. They will grill more quickly than ribs that are not cut flanken style. If you can't find flanken-style short ribs, I recommend slicing regular short ribs nice and thin and then removing the large bones to grill separately.*

LET'S DO IT!

1 Set up the grill for direct grilling. Preheat to 400°F (204°C).

2 Remove the short ribs from the fridge. Remove the ribs from the bag and discard the marinade.

3 Once the coals are white and there is no sign of flames, place the ribs directly on the grill grates. Grill for only about 15 to 30 seconds on one side before flipping them. Continue grilling, moving and flipping them every 15 to 30 seconds, until they develop a golden-brown crust and the internal temperature reaches 165°F (74°C). (This is live-action cooking! You will need to flip and move the ribs frequently to avoid adding grill marks or burning the sugar in the marinade.)

4 Let the ribs rest for 5 to 10 minutes before slicing into individual ribs. Serve warm.

DO IT LIKE GUGA!

It's not always easy cooking direct over coals, but it's better. If you don't get it right the first time, keep trying. I burned quite a few ribs before mastering this technique, but now I can say I make mine perfectly every time, and I enjoy the process of live-action cooking! The secret is to keep moving the ribs continuously. Remember that the marinade contains sugar and you are cooking over a direct fire, which means the marinade can burn quickly.

THE GOD OF STEAKS
JAPANESE WAGYU A5 FILET MIGNON

If there is one steak that should be called "The God of Steaks," this is the one. There is a reason why Japanese Wagyu A5 filet is the most expensive steak per pound you can buy; it's the most tender and most flavorful steak on the planet. And unlike an A5 ribeye or a New York strip, it's enough to satisfy one person and still perfectly balanced, so it's not overwhelming like other A5 steaks. To cook it, you must treat it with great respect!

2 (4oz/115g) Japanese Wagyu A5 filet mignons

Coarse kosher salt

Ground black pepper

PREP AND SEASONING

1 Pat the filets dry using paper towels.

2 Season liberally with kosher salt and black pepper. (You can season before or after cooking, but I recommend seasoning before.)

3 Transfer the steaks to the fridge to rest while you get the grill ready. (Do not let them rest at room temperature. These steaks are small, so it's okay for them to hit the grill cold. The last thing you want is to overcook them! You could eat this steak raw; that's how good it is.)

TIP *To ensure you're getting the real deal, A5 filets will always come with a certificate of authenticity. If you do not receive one of these with your steaks, chances are you are not getting the real deal. The marbling should be amazing! If you can't find A5 filets or they're outside of your budget, you can also use USDA prime filet mignon.*

LET'S DO IT!

1 Set up the grill for two-zone cooking. Preheat to 300°F (149°C). (The grill should be hot, but not extremely hot. If you're cooking with charcoal, there should be no fire and only radiant heat should be emitting from the coals. This will prevent the bitterness that can come from steaks coming into contact with a direct flame.)

2 If there is any residual moisture on the steaks, again pat them dry with paper towels.

3 Place the steaks over direct heat. Sear for 1 minute per side and then flip the steaks. Repeat the process until you've cooked the steaks for 4 minutes total or until they develop a nice golden-brown crust. (There should be no flare-ups. The fat from these steaks is intramuscular, so there will be almost no drippings.)

4 Once the searing process is complete and the steaks reach an internal temperature of 120°F (49°C), remove them from the grill. Set aside to rest for 5 to 10 minutes. (These are small steaks, so the rest time will allow the steaks to reach the final internal temperature of 125°F [52°C].)

5 Slice thinly and enjoy with some sushi rice or a wedge salad. I guarantee this will be an experience you will not forget!

DO IT LIKE GUGA!

If I have multiple steaks, I like to give my guests a different experience by cooking two steaks different ways. I cook them both the same way on the grill, but I'll then make a thyme-garlic butter in a cast-iron pan that's been placed on the hot grill grate. Once the steaks are done searing, I'll transfer one steak to the cast-iron pan to rest in the seasoned butter. I'll then slice the steak, pour the butter over the top, and serve it with the panfried garlic cloves on the side. This is god-like steak! "Amazing" does not sufficiently describe how good it tastes.

WAGYU MS7 NEW YORK STRIP
WITH ROASTED POTATOES

Now let's get a little fancy! Wagyu is the perfect marriage of fat and flavor—and it's not inexpensive, so it's important that you don't mess around with it too much and just keep the seasoning simple. With that said, sometimes the flavor of Wagyu can be a little overwhelming, but not this one! It will be one of the best steaks you've ever tasted, and it's also extremely easy to prepare.

2 (8–12oz/225–340g) Australian Wagyu MS7 New York strip steaks

Coarse kosher salt

Ground black pepper

FOR THE ROASTED POTATOES

1–1½lb (455–680g) mini gold potatoes

2 tbsp olive oil

Smoked paprika

Garlic powder

Coarse kosher salt

Ground black pepper

PREP AND SEASONING

1   Pat the steaks dry with paper towels. Lightly season both sides with kosher salt and black pepper, and then set aside to rest at room temperature while you prep the potatoes.

2   Cut the potatoes into quarters. (This should make them less than 1 inch [2.5cm] thick.)

3   Combine the potatoes and olive oil in a medium bowl. Toss until the potatoes are fully coated with the olive oil, and then season liberally with smoked paprika, garlic powder, kosher salt, and black pepper. Place the potatoes in a single layer on a large sheet pan.

TIP *For an even more tender result and deeper seasoning, try dry brining the steaks overnight prior to grilling. To cut the fattiness of the Wagyu, serve a green salad dressed with red wine vinegar on the side to counterbalance the richness of the steak.*

LET'S DO IT!

1   Preheat the oven to 400°F (204°C). Set up the grill for two-zone cooking. Preheat to 500°F (260°C).

2   Transfer the potatoes to the top rack of the oven. Bake for 25 to 35 minutes or until fork tender.

3   Once the coals are white hot, place the steaks on the grate and directly over the coals. Sear for 30 seconds per side, flipping them frequently, until they have a nice golden-brown color. Once you're happy with the color, move the steaks to the indirect side.

4   Check the internal temperature frequently with a meat thermometer. When the internal temperature reaches 135°F (57°C), transfer the steaks to a plate and then cover with aluminum foil. Set aside to rest for 5 to 10 minutes.

5   Cut the rested steaks into thin strips. Serve with the roasted potatoes on the side.

DO IT LIKE GUGA!

Keep flipping those steaks! Wagyu has a lot of fat, so flare-ups are inevitable. Just flip them as many times as necessary to avoid imparting too much char.

THE KING OF STEAKS
RIBEYE CAP

The "King of Steaks" comes from the ribeye cap, which is considered to be the most flavorful, fatty, and tender part of the ribeye. It's no wonder some people call this "King of Steaks"!

4-bone ribeye roast, chilled

Coarse kosher salt

Ground black pepper

Garlic powder

2 tbsp finely chopped shallots

½ cup crumbled feta

½ cup grated smoked Gouda cheese

2 tbsp chopped Italian parsley

8 tbsp salted butter, melted

PREP AND SEASONING

1 Begin removing the ribeye cap (also known as the *spinalis dorsi*) from the roast by using your fingers to separate it from the eye until you can no longer feel it separating.

2 Using a boning knife, cut the ribeye cap from the rest of the roast. Once you have removed the cap, remove any excess fat and silver skin.

3 Lay the cap flat. Liberally season one side with kosher salt, black pepper, and garlic powder.

4 Sprinkle the shallots, feta, smoked Gouda, and Italian parsley over the seasoned surface. Roll the cap up tightly and then secure it with butcher's twine.

5 Cut the cap into 4 evenly sized steaks and then lightly season the steaks with additional kosher salt, black pepper, and garlic powder.

TIP *Keeping the meat cold will ensure that it doesn't smear during butchering, which will make the job easier.*

LET'S DO IT!

1 Set up the grill for two-zone cooking. Preheat to 250°F (121°C).

2 Place the steaks over indirect heat. Cook for 30 minutes to 1 hour or until the internal temperature reaches 135°F (57°C).

3 When the steaks reach the proper temperature, move them over to the direct-heat side. Sear for about 1 minute per side while basting them continuously with the melted butter until they develop a nice golden-brown crust.

4 Remove the steaks from the grill, and set them aside to rest for 5 to 10 minutes (or as long as you can resist digging into these beautiful steaks!). Remove the butcher's twine, and then slice against the grain to ensure maximum tenderness.

DO IT LIKE GUGA!

Make a quick glaze by reducing balsamic vinegar in a skillet over medium heat. As a rule of thumb, 1 cup of balsamic vinegar should be reduced to about ¼ cup. When you're ready to serve, drizzle some of the balsamic glaze over the top of the steak slices. It's going to be money!

A5 WAGYU RIBEYE

Japanese A5 Wagyu is considered to be the most prestigious meat in the world, and it shows in the price! It should be treated with respect, but don't be afraid to cook it; remember, it's just a steak! So enjoy it! You've worked hard for it!

½ cup short-grain rice

2 tbsp sushi vinegar

10oz (283g) A5 Wagyu ribeye

Coarse kosher salt

Ground black pepper

FOR THE MARINATED EGGS

2 medium eggs

½ cup soy sauce

¼ cup ponzu sauce

1 cup water (or enough to cover the eggs)

1 large white sweet onion, finely diced

4 medium red tomatoes, seeded and finely diced

1 medium green bell pepper, seeded and finely diced

⅓ cup chopped fresh parsley

Coarse kosher salt and ground black pepper, to taste

PREP AND SEASONING

1   Cook the rice according to package instructions. Stir in the sushi vinegar. Set aside.

2   Fill a medium pan with water, and then bring to a boil over high heat. Soft boil the eggs, about 5 minutes, and then remove them from the water to cool. Once cooled, peel the eggs.

3   Combine the soy sauce, ponzu sauce, water, onion, tomatoes, bell pepper, and parsley in a medium bowl. Mix well and then season to taste with kosher salt and black pepper.

4   Submerge the eggs in the marinating mixture. Cover with a paper towel and then place in the fridge to marinate for at least 4 hours (or even better, overnight).

5   Trim any excess fat from the ribeye. (Do not discard the trimmed fat.) Season the meat liberally with kosher salt and black pepper.

TIP *If you have time, prep the marinating mixture the night before cooking so the flavors can meld.*

LET'S DO IT!

1   Set up the grill for direct cooking. Preheat to 350°F (177°C). Place a griddle on the hot grill, and grease the griddle with the trimmed fat from the steak. (Let the griddle get hot!)

2   Place the steak on the hot griddle. Cook for a total of 4 minutes per side, flipping the steak every 30 seconds until it reaches an internal temperature of 135°F to 145°F (57°C to 63°C). (The cooking temperature is up to you. At 135°F the fat will not fully render. The steak will have good flavor but an off mouthfeel. At 145°F, the fat will render more and impart a better mouthfeel for an even more enjoyable steak.)

3   Remove the steak from the griddle and set aside to rest for 5 to 10 minutes before slicing thinly. Divide the sliced steak between two plates. Serve each portion with a scoop of rice and a serving of the marinating mixure topped with a sliced, marinated egg.

DO IT LIKE GUGA!

If you have a rice cooker, use it to cook your rice. Trust me— it's a lot easier and will result in better rice! And if you're feeling fancy, cook up some french fries and serve them on the side to help break up the fattiness of the A5 Wagyu steak!

SMOKED SHORT RIBS
IN STUFFED PASTA SHELLS

Combining pasta and barbecue is something I love to do. This recipe takes a little time to make, but it's absolutely worth the effort!

5lb (2.27kg) short ribs

Coarse kosher salt

Ground black pepper

Garlic powder

12oz (340g) package jumbo pasta shells

6 tbsp grated Parmesan

⅔ cup shredded mozzarella

FOR THE SAUCE

2 cups chopped white onion

3 garlic cloves, minced

2 cups chopped carrots

2 cups chopped celery

2 cups canned diced tomatoes

½ cup red wine

2 cups beef stock

FOR THE FILLING

1½ cups ricotta cheese

1 tbsp chopped fresh parsley

1 tbsp garlic paste

1 tsp cayenne pepper

2 tsp granulated onion

PREP AND SEASONING

1 Remove the silver skin and cap fat from the short ribs. (Doing this will allow you to season them better.) Liberally season the ribs with kosher salt, black pepper, and garlic powder.

2 Make the filling by combining the ricotta cheese, parsley, garlic paste, cayenne pepper, and granulated onion in a medium bowl. Mix well to combine. Transfer to the fridge while the ribs cook.

TIP *For an even more tender result and even better seasoning, try dry brining the short ribs overnight prior to cooking.*

LET'S DO IT!

1 Set up the grill for indirect cooking. Place a heaping handful of hickory wood chunks directly on the coals, and then place a water pan on the grill grates. Preheat the grill to 250°F (121°C).

2 Place the ribs over indirect heat. Cook for about 4 hours or until the internal temperature reaches 175°F (79°C).

3 While the ribs are cooking, prepare the sauce by placing a large skillet over medium heat. Add the onions and sauté until soft, and then add the garlic. Cook until the garlic just begins to caramelize.

4 Add the carrots, celery, and tomatoes. Simmer for 10 minutes, and then add the red wine and beef stock. Continue simmering for an additional 10 minutes.

5 Once the ribs are done cooking, place them in the pan with the sauce. Cover the pan and then place it on the grill for an additional 30 minutes to 1 hour or until the ribs reach an internal temperature of 200°F (93°C) to 205°F (96°C).

6 While the ribs are cooking, cook the pasta shells according to package instructions.

7 Once the meat is fully cooked, remove the pan from the grill and then remove the ribs from the pan. (Don't discard the sauce.) Shred the meat and then add it to the ricotta cheese mixture. Mix well.

8 Strain the sauce through a colander to remove all of the solids. Transfer the strained sauce to a medium pan over medium heat. Simmer until the sauce is reduced by about half.

9 Once the shells are fully cooked, rinse them in cool water and drain. Stuff the cooled shells with the cheese and meat mixture and then place them in a large baking dish.

10 Drizzle some of the sauce over the top of the stuffed shells, and then sprinkle the Parmesan and mozzarella over the top. Place the shells back on the grill just long enough to fully melt the cheese. (Don't let the shells cook for too long or they will become crunchy. You can lightly spray them with water to keep them moist.)

11 Drizzle the rest of that delicious sauce over the shells. Serve warm.

GARLIC BUTTER
CHATEAUBRIAND

This elaborate recipe should be saved for a special day where you can enjoy it with some wine and good company. It's a bit expensive, but it's the perfect dish for the holidays or a special occasion like a birthday dinner. Cured egg yolks and lemon zest add additional color and extra layers of flavor that really make this recipe a showstopper!

2 ½ lb (1.15kg) chateaubriand (center-cut tenderloin)
Coarse kosher salt
Ground black pepper
Garlic powder
7 Cured Egg Yolks (p. 203)
1 tbsp lemon zest

FOR THE GARLIC BUTTER

8 tbsp butter
6 garlic cloves, minced
1 tsp smoked paprika
1 tbsp dried parsley

PREP AND SEASONING

1   Season the chateaubriand liberally with kosher salt, black pepper, and garlic powder. Transfer to the fridge to rest while you make the garlic butter and set up the grill.

2   Begin making the garlic butter by adding the butter to a medium saucepan over medium-low heat. Once the butter is melted, add the garlic, paprika, and parsley. Stir to combine and then remove the saucepan from the heat. Set aside.

LET'S DO IT!

1   Set up the grill for two-zone cooking. Preheat to 250°F (121°C).

2   Place the chateaubriand over indirect heat. Cook for about 1 hour, flipping it occasionally, until it reaches an internal temperature of 120°F (49°C).

3   Move the chateaubriand to the direct-heat side. Sear for about 2 minutes per side while basting continuously with the butter until it develops a nice golden-brown crust on all sides.

4   Transfer the chateaubriand to a cutting board to rest for 5 to 10 minutes.

5   Slice thinly and then place the slices on a serving platter. Drizzle any remaining garlic butter over the top of the slices.

6   Shave the Cured Egg Yolks over the top and then sprinkle the lemon zest over the top. Serve warm.

BEEF
WELLINGTON

Beef Wellington is one of the absolute best holiday meals you can make for your family and friends. Featuring mushroom duxelles, Dijon mustard, Parma ham, and the key ingredient that brings everything together: chateaubriand, which is one of the most flavorful and tender cuts of meat there is. It's no wonder this dish is always a winner!

2lb (907g) chateaubriand (center-cut tenderloin)

Coarse kosher salt

Ground black pepper

Garlic powder

2 large eggs

1 tbsp Dijon mustard

8 slices Parma ham (prosciutto)

2 puff pastry sheets

FOR THE MUSHROOM DUXELLES

1 tsp olive oil

3 cups small portabella mushrooms, chopped

1 tsp garlic paste

1 cup chicken stock

1 tbsp salted butter

Coarse kosher salt and ground black pepper, to taste

TIP *You can also make this recipe in an oven, using the same temperatures and baking times. (It is slightly easier to make it this way.)*

PREP AND SEASONING

1   Season the tenderloin liberally with kosher salt, black pepper, and garlic powder. Tie the tenderloin with butcher's twine to help it keep its shape. Set aside.

2   Make the mushroom duxelles by adding the olive oil to a medium pan over medium heat. Add the mushrooms and sauté until golden brown. Add the garlic paste and chicken stock. Let the ingredients cook until the mushrooms have absorbed all of the chicken stock. Add the butter and stir to combine.

3   Add the mixture to a food processor and process into a paste that is slightly crumbly. Season to taste with kosher salt and black pepper. Set aside.

4   Combine the eggs in a small bowl and whisk with a fork. Set aside.

LET'S DO IT!

1   Set up the grill for two-zone cooking. Preheat to 400°F (204°C). Place a cooling rack on a medium baking tray. Set aside.

2   Remove the butcher's twine from the tenderloin. Place the tenderloin on the direct-heat side. Sear on both sides until it develops a nice golden-brown crust.

3   Remove the seared tenderloin from the grill and immediately brush the Dijon mustard over one side of the tenderloin while it's still hot. Set aside.

4   Place a large sheet of plastic wrap on a flat surface and then arrange the Parma ham slices in a single layer. Spread the mushroom duxelles over the Parma ham slices in a nice, even layer.

5   Place the tenderloin, Dijon mustard side down, on top of the ham slices. Use the plastic wrap to roll everything into a tight cylinder. Transfer to the refrigerator to firm up for 30 minutes. After 30 minutes, remove the tenderloin from the fridge.

6   Place the puff pastry sheets on a sheet of plastic wrap. Unwrap the rolled tenderloin, and place it in the middle of the puff pastry sheets. Roll it into a tight cylinder, and then trim away any excess pastry sheet.

7   Transfer the beef Wellington back to the fridge to rest for 30 more minutes.

8   After 30 minutes, remove the beef Wellington from the fridge. Remove the plastic wrap and place the beef Wellington on a silicone baking mat. Place the beef Wellington and silicone mat on the prepared cooling rack and baking tray.

9   Brush the surface of the beef Wellington with the egg wash and then place it on the grill as far from the heat source as possible. Cook until it reaches an internal temperature of 115°F (46°C). Set aside to rest for 15 to 20 minutes before slicing.

BRAISED SMOKY OSSO BUCCO

Osso bucco is a traditional Italian dish that is usually made with veal shanks. But if you know me, you know I like to put my own twist on things, so I've used beef shanks instead! This recipe is very easy to make and will have your family and friends asking for it again and again!

4 large beef shanks

Coarse kosher salt

Ground black pepper

8 tbsp salted butter, melted

FOR THE SAUCE

2 cups chopped white onion

3 garlic cloves

2 cups chopped carrots

2 cups chopped celery

2 cups canned diced tomatoes

½ cup red wine

2 cups beef stock

PREP AND SEASONING

1   Season the beef shanks liberally with kosher salt and black pepper.

2   Melt the butter in a small saucepan over medium-low heat. Set aside.

TIP *If desired, you can cook this dish the day before serving, store it in the refrigerator overnight, and then reheat it the next day. For some reason I cannot explain, it tastes even better when you reheat it the next day!*

LET'S DO IT!

1   Set up the grill for two-zone cooking. If you're using charcoal, make sure the charcoal is about 4 to 5 inches (10 to 13cm) from the bottom of the grill grate. Preheat the grill to 250°F (121°C).

2   Place the beef shanks on the hot grill and over direct heat. Sear the shanks, turning them frequently while basting them continuously with the melted butter, until they develop a golden-brown color and then remove them from the grill. (You're not fully cooking the meat at this point, you're just giving it a nice sear.)

3   Toss a heaping handful of hickory wood chunks directly into the coals, and then place a water pan on the grill grate.

4   Place the shanks back on the grill over indirect heat. Cook until they reach an internal temperature of 200°F (93°C) to 205°F (96°C), about 3 to 6 hours.

5   While the shanks are cooking, begin preparing the sauce by placing a medium skillet over medium heat. Sauté the onions until soft and then add the garlic cloves. Cook until the garlic cloves just begin to caramelize. (Be careful to not burn them.)

6   Add the carrots, celery, and tomatoes. Simmer for 10 minutes, and then add the red wine and beef stock. Reduce the heat to low, and continue simmering the sauce until the beef shanks are done cooking on the grill.

7   When the beef shanks are done cooking, remove them from the grill. Remove the meat from the bones, and then shred the meat. (Do not discard the bones.)

8   Add the shredded meat and the bones to the skillet with the sauce. Cover the skillet and place it on the grill over indirect heat. Allow the meat and sauce to cook for an additional 30 minutes.

9   Remove and discard the bones. Serve hot. (This is excellent served with Garlic Bread [p. 185] on the side.)

DO IT LIKE GUGA!

This recipe can also be made with short ribs, which will add an even richer beef flavor to the dish.

4-HOUR SMOKED BRISKET

Now we're going to break the rules! This faster brisket method adds additional flavor, and it cooks in about half the time compared to a traditional brisket. The best part is that you have the ability to experiment with the flavoring liquids to add different flavors to the brisket.

½ cup water

½ cup beef stock

½ cup apple cider vinegar

Coarse kosher salt

Ground black pepper

10–15lb (4.5–6.75kg) beef brisket

Yellow mustard or Worcestershire sauce

FOR THE STEAMING LIQUID

1 cup water

1 cup flavoring liquid (wine, Coca-Cola, or whiskey all work great)

1 cup beef stock

1 tbsp coarse kosher salt

PREP AND SEASONING

1   Combine the water, beef stock, and vinegar in a spray bottle. In a small bowl, combine equal amounts of the kosher salt and black pepper. Set aside.

2   For a leaner brisket, trim some of the extra fat from the brisket, leaving ¼ inch (0.65cm) of fat on both the flat and the point. For a brisket that is prime grade or higher, leave ¼ inch (0.65cm) of fat on the flat, but remove all external fat on the point.

3   Rub a very small amount of yellow mustard (or Worcestershire sauce) over the entire brisket. (This will serve as a binder so the seasonings will stick.)

4   Season the entire brisket liberally with the kosher salt and black pepper mixture.

LET'S DO IT!

1   Preheat the smoker to 300°F (149°C). Place a cooling rack on a large baking tray. Set aside.

2   Place the brisket in the smoker. Smoke for 3 hours, spraying the brisket every 30 to 45 minutes with the vinegar–beef stock mixture to prevent a hard, crunchy crust.

3   While the brisket is smoking, make the steaming liquid by combining the water, flavoring liquid, beef stock, and kosher salt in a medium bowl. Stir until the salt is dissolved. Transfer the liquid to the prepared baking pan. Set aside.

4   After 3 hours, check the brisket. If the color is to your liking, place the brisket on the cooling rack and baking pan with the seasoning liquid. Cover the brisket and baking tray with a large sheet of aluminum foil.

5   Place the brisket and baking tray back in the smoker. Continue smoking for an additional 1 to 2 hours or until the internal temperature reaches 200°F (93°C) to 205°F (96°C) and there is very little resistance when you poke the brisket with a toothpick.

6   Remove the brisket from the smoker and set it aside to rest for at least 1 hour or up to 5 hours. (The longer, the better.) If desired, place the brisket in a cooler or an oven set to 150°F (66°C) to help keep it warm.

7   Slice the rested brisket against the grain and into thin slices. Serve warm.

DRY-BRINED SMOKED SHORT RIBS

This variation breaks the Texas-style rule and adds more flavor! Note there is no salt in the rub. That's because you'll be dry brining the ribs overnight.

5–10lb (2.25–4.5kg) short ribs

Coarse kosher salt

FOR THE RUB

2 tbsp granulated garlic

2 tbsp ground black pepper

1 tbsp granulated onion

1 tbsp celery salt

1 tbsp smoked paprika

1 tsp dry mustard

1 tsp cayenne pepper

2 tsp Homemade MSG Seasoning (p. 217) or store-bought MSG seasoning

PREP AND SEASONING

1   Place the ribs on a large tray with a cooling rack. Cover completely in kosher salt, and then transfer to the fridge to dry brine overnight.

2   Combine the rub ingredients in a medium bowl. Set aside.

3   Pat the dry-brined ribs dry with paper towels. (If needed, dampen the paper towels to remove as much of the juices as possible from the bones.)

4   Use a sharp knife to remove most of the external top fat to expose the meat. (This will allow the rub to better penetrate the meat.)

5   Remove the silver skin layer from the meat, but don't remove the silver skin from the bones. (Doing so can compromise the structure of the short ribs when smoking.)

6   Liberally season the ribs with the rub.

LET'S DO IT!

1   Preheat the smoker to 275°F (135°C). Once the smoker reaches temperature, wait 20 minutes before adding the short ribs.

2   Place the short ribs in the smoker and as far away from the heat source as possible. (The goal is to get smoke on the ribs, but not to fully cook them at this point.)

3   Smoke for 4 hours or until the ribs develop a nice golden-brown color.

4   After 4 hours, wrap the ribs to finish the cook. For a faster cook (1 to 3 hours) and an extremely soft bark, wrap the ribs in aluminum foil, being extra careful not to damage the bark. For a dryer bark and a longer cook (3 to 5 hours), wrap the ribs in butcher paper. Place the wrapped ribs back in the smoker.

5   After 1 to 2 hours, poke the meat with a toothpick. If it feels like a knife going through room-temperature butter, use a meat thermometer to check the temperature. If the temperature is 200°F (93°C) to 205°F (96°C), the ribs are done cooking. If the ribs are not at temperature, place them back in the smoker and check them every 45 minutes to 1 hour until they are done.

6   Remove the ribs from the smoker. Set aside to rest in a closed container like a cold oven or cooler for a minimum of 1 hour and up to 4 hours, letting them rest for no longer than 4 hours. (If you need to let the ribs rest for longer than 4 hours, set your oven to the lowest setting and place the fully wrapped ribs in the oven for up to 10 hours.)

7   Slice into individual ribs. Serve warm. (Always serve with the bones, as one of the most amazing parts of short ribs is the crispy skin that is left on the bones.)

POULTRY

POULTRY

In this section you'll learn about the different cuts of poultry eaten in the US, how they are used, and how to buy the highest quality poultry.

THE CUTS

When it comes to poultry, there are three main cuts. In different places around the world, they use every part of the bird, including feet, neck, hearts, or even the whole carcass, but for the sake of barbeque, we tend to stick to the wings, thighs, and breasts.

Wings Chicken wings are hands-down the best party food there is! I love them fried, I love them baked, and I definitely loved them grilled! They are so flavorful and there are so many ways you can add flavor to wings and make them your own, which is why they are possibly the most popular cut of chicken.

Thighs I like chicken thighs better than chicken breasts because of the amount of fat and flavor they have. They have to be cooked a little bit longer than breasts to ensure they come out nice and tender, but there are endless ways you can cook thighs and so many different dishes you can use them in.

Breasts I don't like chicken breasts as much as chicken thighs because they are drier and have less fat, but surprisingly, they are the more popular cut of the two. Cooked right, however, they can still be delicious. As a general rule, I only like to use chicken breasts if I'm in a rush, because they cook faster than thighs.

WHAT TO LOOK FOR WHEN BUYING POULTRY

Poultry is not like beef or pork: there is no marbling in the meat that can help you determine the quality of the cut, and as a general rule, most breeds do not vary when it comes to flavor. However, when buying poultry, there are still some things to keep in mind.

Grading Poultry grading in the US is pretty simple: packages will be labeled as either grade A, grade B, or grade C. Grade A is what you'll find in US supermarkets, and it's the highest quality of the three and should be the only grade you buy. It's uncommon to find Grades B and C in supermarkets. As a general rule, you can buy either fresh or frozen poultry without any difference in taste.

Organic When buying poultry, look for organic options. Many supermarkets will inject poultry with a brining solution that makes the meat look plumper. This process dilutes the flavor of the meat. By buying organic chicken, you can be assured that the meat has not been injected with anything and you'll have fresh, better-tasting meat.

POULTRY

THE RECIPES

JERK CHICKEN FROM HEAVEN

Chicken can be boring if isn't prepared properly. But if you use the right seasoning and cook it the right way, you can make it into an incredible dish. Trust me, this jerk chicken doesn't suck! It's as good as it gets!

4–5lb (1.8–2.25kg) organic whole chicken

Coarse kosher salt

FOR THE JERK MARINADE

1 medium white onion, coarsely chopped

3 medium scallions, chopped

2 Scotch bonnet chiles, chopped

2 garlic cloves, chopped

1 tbsp five spice powder

1 tbsp allspice berries, coarsely ground

1 tbsp coarsely ground black pepper

1 tsp dried thyme

1 tsp freshly grated nutmeg

1 tsp salt

½ cup soy sauce

1 tbsp vegetable oil

FOR THE BBQ SAUCE

1 tbsp olive oil

1 tbsp chopped shallots

1 tbsp minced ginger

2 garlic cloves, minced

7 tbsp ketchup

2 tbsp jerk marinade

PREP AND SEASONING

1   Remove the giblets and pat the chicken dry with paper towels. Cut the chicken into individual pieces (breasts, drumsticks, thighs, wings, and wing tips).

2   Carefully loosen the skin and generously season the meat underneath with kosher salt. (For smaller pieces like the wings, the marinade will do the job just fine.) Set aside.

3   Prepare the marinade by combining the ingredients in a blender. Blend on high until the ingredients are finely chopped and the consistency is similar to that of a marinade.

4   Place the chicken pieces in a large resealable freezer bag. Reserve 2 tablespoons of the marinade for the sauce, and then add the remaining marinade to the bag with the chicken. Seal and gently rotate to coat the chicken pieces with the marinade. Place the bag in a large bowl, and place it in the fridge to marinate for 24 hours.

5   Make the BBQ sauce by adding the olive oil to a large frying pan over medium heat. When the oil is shimmering, add the shallots, ginger, and garlic. Sauté just until fragrant. (Do not let the ingredients brown.)

6   Add the ketchup and reserved marinade. Cook over medium-low heat until the sauce is fragrant, about 2 minutes. Transfer to a blender and blend on high until smooth. Set aside to cool. Once cool, transfer to a resealable container and place in the fridge until you're ready to cook.

LET'S DO IT!

1   Set up the grill for two-zone cooking. Preheat to 375°F (191°C).

2   Remove the chicken from the fridge and discard the marinade. Remove the BBQ sauce from the fridge and set aside.

3   Place the chicken over indirect heat. Cook the chicken for 30 minutes, flipping the pieces every 10 minutes to ensure even cooking.

4   After 30 minutes, begin very lightly brushing the chicken with the barbecue sauce every 10 minutes, being careful not to brush so hard as to remove the spices from the surface of the chicken. Continue cooking for another 20 to 30 minutes or until the internal temperature reaches 165°F (74°C) for white meat pieces and 175°F (79°C) for dark meat pieces.

5   Allow to rest for 10 to 15 minutes. Serve hot.

EASY BBQ CHICKEN THIGHS

These chicken thighs are so simple to make, yet they're just amazing! The key is cooking the thighs the right way and adding just the right amount of flavor by combining traditional seasonings, BBQ sauce, melted butter, and most importantly—that smoky flavor from the charcoal!

5lb (2.25kg) skin-on or skinless chicken thighs

2 tbsp olive oil

Coarse kosher salt

4 tbsp Guga's BBQ Rub (p. 200)

3–4 tbsp butter, melted

½ cup Guga's BBQ Sauce (p. 201)

PREP AND SEASONING

1 Pat the thighs dry with paper towels. Trim away any excess fat.

2 Lightly brush the thighs with the olive oil, and then season lightly with kosher salt.

3 Sprinkle Guga's BBQ Rub over the thighs to coat all sides.

4 Transfer the thighs to a plate, and then place them in the fridge while you set up the grill.

TIP *For even more amazing flavor, try brining the thighs overnight in buttermilk and then dry brining them for an additional 8 to 12 hours in the fridge. The entire process can take up to 24 hours, but it will be even better in the end! You can also lightly season the thighs with MSG seasoning prior to cooking.*

LET'S DO IT!

1 Set up the grill for two-zone cooking. Preheat to 350°F (177°C). (You can also cook these in the smoker.)

2 Place the thighs over indirect heat. Cook for approximately 1 hour, basting the thighs occasionally with the melted butter, until the internal temperature reaches 175°F (79°C). (In my opinion, chicken thighs taste better when the internal temperature is a little higher than the standard 165°F [74°C].)

3 Transfer the thighs to the direct-heat side. Sear for 1 to 2 minutes, turning them frequently, just until the skin is crisped. (If you're making these in the smoker, you can use a torch to crisp the skin or you can crisp the skin under the oven broiler.)

4 Remove the thighs from the grill, and brush with the BBQ sauce. Place the thighs back on the grill for 2 to 4 more minutes to set the sauce.

5 Remove the thighs from the grill. Tightly cover with aluminum foil, and then set aside to rest for 5 minutes before serving.

DO IT LIKE GUGA!

For the ultimate crispy chicken skin, deep-fry the thighs before cooking them in the smoker. Use Wagyu fat to fry, and set the oil temperature to 400°F (204°C). Deep-fry the thighs for 2 to 4 minutes. By the time the chicken is done cooking, you will have the ultimate crispy skin and a deep smoky flavor!

SMOKED CHICKEN STROGANOFF

My family and I eat this dish at least once a week! Whenever I say I'm cooking chicken, the follow-up question is always, "Is it stroganoff?" They all love this recipe, especially if I serve it with shoestring potato fries and pair it with steamed rice. Don't underestimate the power of this recipe! It's that good!

3lb (1.35kg) boneless, skinless chicken breasts

Coarse kosher salt

Ground black pepper

Granulated garlic

1 tbsp chopped fresh parsley, for garnishing

FOR THE SAUCE

3 tbsp butter

1 cup diced white onion

1 garlic clove, crushed

1 (15oz/425g) can tomato sauce

1 tbsp Worcestershire sauce

2 tbsp ketchup

1 tbsp yellow mustard

2 (7.6fl oz/225mL) cans table cream, drained

Coarse kosher salt, to taste

FOR THE BASTING SPRAY

½ cup red wine vinegar

1½ cups water

PREP AND SEASONING

1   Make the basting spray by combining the red wine vinegar and water in a spray bottle. Set aside.

2   Pat the chicken breasts dry with paper towels. Trim away any external fat.

3   Liberally season the chicken breasts with kosher salt, black pepper, and granulated garlic.

4   Place the chicken breasts on a plate, and then transfer to the fridge while you prepare the sauce.

5   Begin preparing the sauce by placing a medium saucepan over medium heat. Add the butter. When the butter is melted, add the onion. Sauté until golden brown, and then add the garlic. Sauté for 1 minute more.

6   Add the tomato sauce and cook for 1 minute, and then add the Worcestershire sauce, ketchup, and mustard. Stir to combine and then add the table cream.

7   Reduce the heat to low and cook, stirring continuously, until the cream is incorporated and the sauce is hot. (The milk solids can separate if you don't keep stirring.) Season to taste with kosher salt.

TIP *You can double or even triple this recipe and store it in your fridge for up to a week. Just reheat it in the microwave. A kettle grill also will work for smoking the chicken; just be sure to cook over indirect heat, and also add a heaping handful of wood chunks to the coals.*

LET'S DO IT!

1   Preheat the smoker to 250°F (121°C).

2   Place the chicken breasts in the smoker. Smoke for 30 to 45 minutes or until the internal temperature reaches 165°F (74°C), spraying the chicken breasts every 10 minutes with the vinegar-water solution.

3   When the chicken breasts are done cooking, transfer them to a cutting board to rest for 10 minutes.

4   Chop the rested chicken breasts into chunks. Transfer the chopped chicken to 4 to 5 serving bowls, and then spoon the sauce over the top. Toss to coat and then garnish with the parsley. Serve hot.

DO IT LIKE GUGA!

I use this same sauce for steak stroganoff. The recipe is the same, but instead of chicken breasts I use grilled skirt steaks. This recipe can also be made with pork loin.

BUTTER CHICKEN
FROM THE GODS

I've made some amazing chicken recipes in my lifetime, but this one is something special! The taste is just crazy good; it's one of those recipes that *everyone* loves. The best part is that the gravy can be made ahead of time, which makes things so easy.

4lb (1.80kg) boneless, skinless chicken thighs

Coarse kosher salt

Ground black pepper

Kashmiri chili powder

1 tbsp garlic paste

1 tbsp ground ginger

1 tbsp heavy cream, for drizzling

Pinch of dried parsley, for garnishing

FOR THE GRAVY

8 tbsp butter

7oz (200g) roughly chopped white onions

1–2 tbsp garlic paste

28oz (800g) roughly chopped tomatoes

2.75oz (80g) cashew nuts

4 tbsp granulated sugar

1 tsp garam masala

2 tbsp malt vinegar

1½ tbsp white vinegar

3 tbsp Kashmiri chili powder

Kosher salt and ground black pepper, to taste

6 tbsp heavy cream

PREP AND SEASONING

1   Pat the chicken thighs dry with paper towels.

2   Liberally season the thighs with kosher salt, and then lightly season with black pepper and Kashmiri chili powder.

3   In a small bowl, combine the garlic paste and ground ginger. Stir to combine and then brush the paste onto the thighs. Place the thighs in a large bowl, cover with plastic wrap, and then place in the fridge to marinate for 24 hours.

4   While the thighs are marinating, prepare the gravy. Add the butter to a deep skillet over medium-low heat. Once the butter is melted, adjust the heat to medium and add the onions. Sauté the onions for 5 to 10 minutes, stirring occasionally, until browned, and then add the garlic paste. Stir to combine.

5   Add the tomatoes, cashews, sugar, garam masala, malt vinegar, white vinegar, and Kashmiri chili powder. Mix well and then cook for about 10 minutes. Season to taste with kosher salt and black pepper.

6   Add the heavy cream and stir. Use an immersion blender to blend until smooth. (Alternatively, transfer the ingredients to a blender and blend until smooth.)

7   Using a fine mesh strainer, strain the gravy into a large bowl. Discard the solids. (The result should be a very smooth gravy.)

8   Cover the bowl and transfer the gravy to the fridge until ready to use.

TIP *You can double or even triple the gravy recipe. (It freezes perfectly.) When you want to make butter chicken, just warm the gravy in a water bath or sous vide bath at 140°F (60°F) for 30 minutes.*

LET'S DO IT!

1   Set up the grill for two-zone cooking. Preheat to 350°F (177°C). Remove the chicken and gravy from the fridge.

2   Place the chicken over direct heat. Sear the chicken, turning it frequently, until it develops a golden-brown color. (Don't sear the thighs for too long; you don't want to cook them completely at this stage.)

3   Move the chicken to indirect heat. Cook until the internal temperature reaches 175°F (79°C).

4   Add the gravy to a medium pan over medium heat. Heat the sauce until warmed through, and then remove from the heat.

5   Transfer the chicken to a cutting board. Allow to rest for 5 to 10 minutes, and then chop into small, bite-sized pieces. Transfer the chicken along with the juices from the cutting board to a deep serving dish. Spoon the gravy over the top.

6   Drizzle 1 tablespoon heavy cream over the top and then garnish with a pinch of dried parsley. (This dish is excellent served with steamed white rice on the side.)

NASHVILLE HOT FRIED TURKEY BREAST

I don't like turkey as much as I like chicken. But when I do choose turkey, it's because of this recipe! The spicy kick and perfect sweetness, combined with the juicy, tender turkey breast, is next-level stuff!

6lb (2.75kg) turkey breast

8 tbsp unsalted butter

4 cups plus 2 to 3 tbsp Wagyu tallow (or equal amount of avocado oil), divided

FOR THE MARINADE

2 cups buttermilk

6 tbsp Louisiana-style hot sauce (I like Crystal brand)

1 tbsp coarse kosher salt

1 tbsp smoked paprika

1 tbsp garlic powder

2 medium eggs

FOR THE SPICY SEASONING OIL

10 tbsp cayenne pepper

8 tbsp brown sugar

2 tbsp black pepper

2 tbsp garlic powder

2 tbsp smoked paprika

1½ cups reserved hot cooking oil

FOR THE FLOUR MIX

1 cup all-purpose flour

½ tbsp coarse kosher salt

½ tbsp smoked paprika

½ tbsp ground black pepper

½ tbsp garlic powder

PREP AND SEASONING

1   Pat the turkey breast dry with paper towels. Use a deboning knife to remove any bones by following the contour of the breast bone with the knife, staying as close as possible to the bone and removing as much meat as possible, while still keeping the breast intact.

2   In a large bowl, combine the marinade ingredients and mix well. Reserve one-third of the marinade in a medium bowl. Cover and transfer to the fridge. Place the turkey breast in the large bowl with the remaining marinade. Cover and transfer to the fridge to marinate for 24 to 48 hours.

3   Make the flour mix by combining all of the ingredients in a medium bowl. Cover and set aside.

4   Once the marinating time for the turkey breast is complete, remove the turkey breast from the marinade, but don't pat it dry.

5   Melt the butter in a small pan placed over medium-low heat. Inject 4 tablespoons of the melted butter into each side of the marinated turkey breast. Set aside while you get the smoker ready.

LET'S DO IT!

1   Preheat the smoker to 250°F (121°C). Remove the reserved marinade and seasoning oil from the fridge. Set aside.

2   Place the turkey breast in the smoker. Smoke for approximately 1 hour or until the internal temperature reaches 165°F (74°C).

3   While the turkey breast is smoking, place the bowls with the reserved marinade and flour mix on a flat surface.

4   When the turkey breast is done cooking, remove it from the smoker. Dip it into the reserved marinade followed by the flour mix. Repeat the process once, and then set the turkey breast aside on a cooling rack.

5   Heat 4 cups of the Wagyu tallow to 400°F (204°C) in a deep fryer or large pot.

6   Very carefully place the turkey breast in the hot oil. Fry just until a golden crust is achieved, about 2 to 4 minutes. Transfer the breast to a cooling rack and turn off the burner.

7   Begin making the spicy seasoning oil by combining the spicy seasoning oil dry seasonings in a medium bowl. Add the remaining 2 to 3 tablespoons of cold Wagyu tallow to the hot cooking oil to bring down the temperature. Stir. Once the temperature of the oil reaches between 325°F (163°C) and 350°F (177°C), carefully transfer 1½ cups of the hot cooking oil to the bowl with the seasonings. Stir. (Make sure the Wagyu oil is no hotter than 350°F [177°C]. If it's too hot, the sugar will burn and impart a bitter taste to the oil.)

8   Liberally brush the seasoning oil onto the turkey breast, coating all sides. (How heavily you coat the turkey with the oil is up to you.)

9   Set aside to rest for 5 to 10 minutes. Slice and serve with some soft white bread and mashed potatoes on the side. (I guarantee this will be the best turkey breast you've ever tasted!)

DO IT LIKE GUGA!

It's extremely important that your Wagyu fat is quite hot when you fry the turkey breast. If you don't flash fry the turkey breast and cook it for too long, you'll likely overcook it, and that's not what we want. So, make sure the oil is 400°F (204°C) before you add the turkey, and don't flash fry it for longer than 4 minutes.

DO IT LIKE GUGA!

If the skin gets too sticky, it may be because you're using lower-quality chicken thighs. I recommend using organic chicken thighs, which will have less fat than conventional chicken thighs. If the fat under the skin isn't rendering properly, that's likely why they are sticking to the grates. If they do get stuck, try using a fish spatula to remove them, and do all you can not to damage the skin because that will be the best part!

GRILLED LEMON CHICKEN THIGHS

Stop eating boring chicken! These thighs are not only easy to make, they have incredible flavor and can even be made into a weeknight meal if you want to shorten the marinating time. If anyone in your family doesn't like chicken, I promise this one will be a winner winner chicken dinner with them!

3lb to 5lb (1.35kg to 2.25kg) skin-on chicken thighs

2–3 sprigs fresh rosemary, divided

Sprig of fresh thyme

8 tbsp salted butter

2 tbsp Guga's BBQ Rub (p. 200), divided

5 medium lemons

FOR THE MARINADE

4 tbsp olive oil

3 garlic cloves, minced

4 tbsp red wine vinegar

1 tbsp soy sauce

1 tbsp salt

2 tbsp Dijon mustard

1 tbsp sriracha sauce

TIP *You can use a vacuum sealer or vacuum chamber to speed up the marinating process. The marinade will penetrate deeper and the chicken will taste even better!*

PREP AND SEASONING

1   Pat the thighs dry with paper towels. Trim away any excess fat, but leave the skin intact. Set aside.

2   Combine the marinade ingredients in a large bowl. Whisk until well combined.

3   Place the chicken thighs in the bowl with the marinade, toss to coat the thighs in the marinade. Cover and transfer to the fridge to marinate overnight or up to 10 hours. (Marinating overnight will yield the best flavor, but if you're in a hurry, you can reduce the marinating time to 1 to 2 hours.)

4   When the marinating time is complete, remove the thighs from the marinade and place them skin sides down on a cooling rack. Set aside.

5   Prep the basting "brush" by using butcher's twine to tie a rosemary sprig and thyme sprig to the brush end of a regular basting brush.

6   Make a basting butter by adding the butter and 1 tablespoon of Guga's BBQ Rub in a small bowl. Microwave it until the butter is melted. Stir.

7   Season only the flesh sides with the remaining 1 tablespoon of Guga's BBQ Rub. (The thighs should be nice and wet with the marinade, so the rub should stick well. Do not season the skin sides.)

8   Place the thighs in the fridge while you get the grill ready.

LET'S DO IT!

1   Set up the grill for two-zone cooking. Preheat to 400°F (204°C). Cut the lemons in half and set them aside.

2   Place the chicken thighs, skin sides down, over indirect heat. Cook for 15 minutes, and then open the lid and use the herb "brush" to baste the thighs with the basting butter.

3   Carefully flip the thighs to be skin sides up. Grill for an additional 10 to 15 minutes or until the internal temperature reaches 175°F (79°C). (If the skin is sticking to the grill grates, give the thighs another 5 to 10 minutes on the grill and they should release.)

4   When the thighs reach temperature, move them to the direct heat side and sear for 1 minute per side. Keep flipping them until they are nice and golden brown. (A little char is okay.) Transfer to a serving platter.

5   Place the lemon halves over the indirect heat and grill until they develop nice grill marks. Transfer to the platter with the chicken thighs.

6   Set aside to rest for 5 to 10 minutes. Garnish with the remaining rosemary twigs. (Encourage your guests to squeeze as much lemon juice as they desire over the chicken because it will be very delicious!)

JALAPEÑO CRUST
CHICKEN CORDON BLEU

This quick and delicious twist on traditional chicken cordon bleu is a recipe your entire family will love. This was one of my favorite dishes when I was a kid. And while I might have discovered steak as I got older, this remains one of my family's favorite recipes!

4 large boneless, skinless chicken breasts

4 slices thinly sliced deli ham (about ¼lb [114g])

4 slices mozzarella cheese (about ½lb [227g])

Coarse kosher salt

Ground black pepper

4 slices uncooked bacon

1 medium jalapeño, seeded and diced

1 tbsp fresh minced parsley

2 cups unseasoned bread crumbs

2 cups all-purpose flour

2 large eggs

4 cups avocado oil

FOR THE SAUCE

4 tbsp butter

2 tbsp all-purpose flour

1 cup cold whole milk

½ cup grated Parmesan cheese

1 tsp Dijon mustard

Salt and white pepper, to taste

PREP AND SEASONING

1   Butterfly the chicken breasts. Stuff each breast with a slice of ham and a slice of cheese. Fold the chicken breasts closed and then season liberally with kosher salt and black pepper. Place on a plate and then transfer to the fridge.

2   Place a medium skillet over medium-low heat. Add the bacon and fry until it's nice and crispy. Transfer to a paper towel–lined plate to drain.

3   Combine the bacon, jalapeño, parsley, and bread crumbs in a food processor. Process until well combined and a crumbly texture is achieved. Transfer to a shallow baking dish.

LET'S DO IT!

1   Place the all-purpose flour in a shallow dish. Whisk the eggs in a separate shallow dish.

2   Dredge the chicken breasts in the flour, dip them in the egg wash, and then coat them in the jalapeño bread crumbs. Place on a plate and set aside until you're ready to cook.

3   Begin making the sauce by melting the butter in a large saucepan over medium heat. When the butter is melted, add the flour and mix well. Stir continuously until the mixture develops a nice buttery smell and a light brown color, about 4 to 5 minutes.

4   Add the cold milk while continuing to stir, and then add the Parmesan cheese and Dijon mustard. Continue stirring until the sauce is smooth and hot. (If the sauce is too thick, add a bit more milk.) Season to taste with salt and white pepper. Remove from the heat and set aside.

5   Place a large, deep skillet over medium-high heat. Add the avocado oil and heat to 325°F (163°C).

6   When the oil is hot, carefully add the chicken breasts. Fry until the chicken reaches an internal temperature of 165°F (74°C). Transfer the chicken breasts to a paper towel–lined plate to rest for 5 to 10 minutes.

7   Transfer the chicken breasts to a serving platter, and then drizzle the sauce over the top. Serve hot.

FLAMING TAKIS SMOKED CHICKEN THIGHS

You've probably had traditional fried chicken thighs, but I'm willing to bet you've never tried anything like this! These thighs are spicy, smoky, and easy to make, but most importantly, they're delicious! Give these a try and I guarantee you'll never look at chicken the same again.

5 bone-in, skinless chicken thighs

1 tsp coarse kosher salt

1 cup buttermilk

1 (9.9oz/281g) bag Fuego Takis

Canola or peanut oil, for frying

FOR THE SEASONING BLEND

⅔ tsp coarse kosher salt

½ tsp dried thyme

½ tsp dried basil

⅓ tsp dried oregano

1 tsp celery salt

1 tsp black pepper

1 tsp dried mustard

4 tsp smoked paprika

2 tsp granulated garlic

1 tsp ground ginger

3 tsp white pepper

¾ tsp Homemade MSG Seasoning (p. 217) or store-bought MSG seasoning

PREP AND SEASONING

1 Make the seasoning blend by combining all the ingredients in a medium bowl. Stir until well combined.

2 Season the thighs with the coarse kosher salt, and then coat with the seasoning blend. Put the seasoned thighs in a large bowl, and then pour the buttermilk over the the top. Cover the bowl and transfer the chicken to the fridge to marinate overnight.

3 Working in batches, add the Takis to a food processor. Process until the Takis form a fine powder. Place in a shallow dish, cover, and set aside.

LET'S DO IT!

1 Preheat the smoker to 400°F (204°C).

2 Remove the chicken thighs from the fridge. Shake very gently to remove any excess buttermilk, and then dredge in the Takis powder. Shake very gently to remove any excess powder, and then place the thighs on a cooling rack.

3 Place a large cast-iron skillet over medium-high heat. Add the oil to the skillet and heat to 350°F (177°C). Carefully place the thighs in the hot oil. Fry just until they develop a nice golden-brown color, about 2 minutes, flipping them halfway through the cooking process. Remove the thighs from the oil and place them on a cooling rack.

4 Place the thighs in the smoker. Smoke for 30 minutes to 1 hour or until they reach an internal temperature of 175°F (79°C).

5 Set aside to rest for 5 to 10 minutes. Serve hot.

DO IT LIKE GUGA!

If you want to take these to the next level, try frying the chicken thighs in Wagyu beef tallow. It will give the chicken an incredible flavor and really take it over the top!

TERIYAKI CHICKEN THIGHS

No need to order takeout anymore now that you have this recipe in your arsenal! Making these addicting chicken thighs at home is so incredibly easy. The teriyaki sauce for this recipe is so good, you can add it to any dish and it will turn out amazing.

6 skinless chicken thighs

Coarse kosher salt

Ground black pepper

Garlic powder

8 tbsp butter

1 tbsp Guga's BBQ Rub (p. 200)

2 tbsp toasted sesame seeds

FOR THE TERIYAKI SAUCE

1 tbsp olive oil

8 garlic cloves, minced

2 tbsp minced fresh ginger root

3 tbsp dark soy sauce

1 tbsp sugar

5 tbsp mirin (rice wine)

3 tbsp sake

½ tbsp cornstarch

2 tbsp water

PREP AND SEASONING

1   Season the chicken thighs liberally with kosher salt, black pepper, and garlic powder. Place the thighs on a plate, cover with plastic wrap, and then transfer to the fridge until you're ready to cook.

2   Begin making the teriyaki sauce by adding the olive oil to a medium saucepan over low heat. Add the garlic and ginger root. Cook until the garlic and ginger root become fragrant, about 1 minute.

3   Add the dark soy sauce, sugar, mirin, and sake. Stir to combine and then bring to a simmer.

4   Combine the cornstarch and water in a small bowl. Stir to make a slurry. (This will help thicken the sauce.) Add the slurry to the sauce and stir to combine. Continue simmering until the liquid reaches a sauce-like consistency. Remove from the heat and set aside.

5   Add the butter and Guga's BBQ Rub to a small saucepan over medium-low heat. Heat until the butter is melted, stir, and then remove the pan from the heat. Set aside.

TIP   *You can make the sauce ahead of time. It will last in your refrigerator for up to 1 week, and you can use it for several different dishes.*

LET'S DO IT!

1   Set up the grill for indirect cooking. Preheat to 375°F (191°C)

2   Place the chicken thighs over indirect heat. Grill for about 1 hour, turning them occasionally and basting them with the seasoned butter every 10 minutes for the first 40 minutes of cooking time.

3   For the last 20 minutes of cooking time, baste the thighs with the teriyaki sauce every 10 minutes, turning them frequently, until the thighs reach an internal temperature of 175°F (79°C).

4   Remove the chicken thighs from the grill. Glaze them once more with the teriyaki sauce, and then sprinkle the toasted sesame seeds over the top.

5   Set aside to rest for 5 to 10 minutes. Serve warm.

KOREAN-STYLE CHICKEN WINGS

Forget about carryout chicken wings! This recipe will have you making wings that are better than anything you can ever get from a restaurant. These are absolutely perfect for a tailgate or a family barbecue. I guarantee everyone will love them!

50 chicken wings (fresh or frozen)

Zest of 1 medium lemon

1 tbsp chopped scallions

2 tsp toasted sesame seeds

FOR THE MARINADE

1 cup minced white onion

1 cup garlic paste

1 cup gochujang paste

½ cup grated fresh ginger root

½ cup chili pepper flakes

1 cup honey

1 cup soy sauce

½ cup granulated sugar

PREP AND SEASONING

1   Make the marinade by combining the onion, garlic paste, gochujang paste, ginger root, chili pepper flakes, honey, soy sauce, and sugar in a medium bowl. Mix well.

2   Add the wings to a large bowl. Working in batches, pour half of the marinade over the top of the wings and toss to ensure the wings are well coated in the marinade. (Reserve the remaining half of the marinade for brushing during grilling.)

3   Grate the lemon zest over the top of the wings and then toss again. Let the wings marinate in the refrigerator for at least 3 hours.

TIP   *If you're using frozen chicken wings, allow them to defrost in the fridge overnight prior to marinating.*

LET'S DO IT!

1   Set up the grill for indirect cooking. Preheat to 400°F (204°C).

2   Working in batches if needed, place the wings over indirect heat. Grill for about 45 minutes, brushing frequently with the reserved marinade, until the wings reach an internal temperature of 180°F (82°C).

3   Transfer the wings to a serving platter. Sprinkle the scallions and sesame seeds over the top.

4   Set aside to rest for 5 to 10 minutes. Serve warm.

DO IT LIKE GUGA!

If desired, you can let the wings marinate overnight for an even better and more intense flavor.

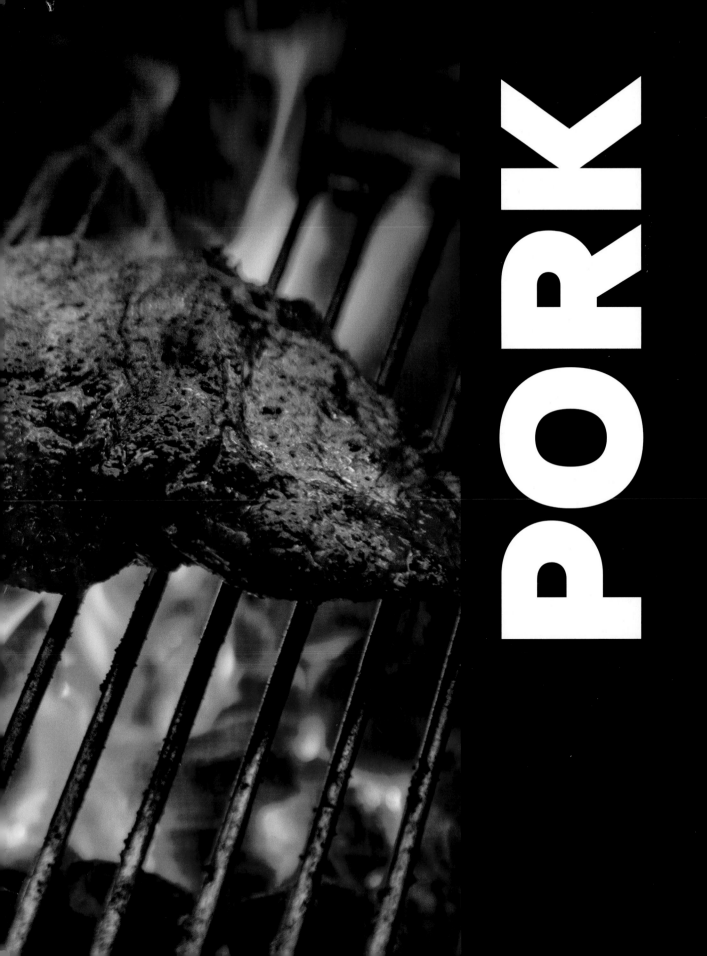

PORK

MEET THE MEAT

PORK

Pork is the most widely eaten meat in the world, and for good reason: it's delicious! In this section you'll learn about the different cuts, different breeds, and what makes pork taste so good. I'll even explain to you the different pork grades and what to look for when buying pork to ensure you get the best of the best.

THE CUTS

These are the most common cuts and the different meats in each cut.

Ham The number one reason pork is the top-selling meat is ham! Ham has been one of my favorite things to eat for as long as I can remember. There are several different variations of ham that can be found across the world.

Loin Pork loin is one of the trickiest things to cook; if it's done right, it can be extremely juicy and flavorful, but if it's done wrong, it can be very dry and flavorless. You have to make sure you cook this meat to the perfect temperature to get the best out of it.

Belly Pork belly is the best part of the pig. Why? Because it's where bacon comes from! And let's be honest: who doesn't love bacon? Steak might be my favorite meat, but pork belly is a very close second!

Arm Shoulder The arm shoulder is where picnic pork comes from; it's the perfect meat for the Latin dish lechon because it usually comes with skin on, which makes it perfect for making that crackling that everyone loves.

Blade Shoulder Boston butt comes from the blade shoulder. This is what is used for traditional American-style slow BBQ. It's perfect for BBQ pulled pork and other amazing dishes!

Ribs If I invite you to my house to eat, you had better be ready to have some pork ribs. Pork ribs are one of my favorite things to cook and are always what my guests remember the most!

WHAT MAKES GOOD PORK?

Good pork is a combination of good meat with the right ratio of fat. When you buy pork, you'll want to buy nice, even cuts so they cook evenly, but there are other factors that have an impact on the quality of the pork you buy.

Breed Breeding is important when it comes to pork just like it is for beef. Different breeds of pork produce different meats, with several different flavors. Yorkshire is the most common breed used in most BBQ joints, whereas Iberico—considered to be the Wagyu of pork—has an entirely different flavor and is less common because it's much more expensive.

Diet What a pig eats is important because it can change and affect the flavor and texture of the meat. Iberico pigs eat mostly acorns, which gives the meat a rich, nutty flavor. Yorkshire pigs, however, eat a lot of fruits, vegetables, and even leftover food scraps, which yield a different flavor and also help them get big and plump.

Marbling Another thing to look for is good intramuscular marbling, just like when you buy beef, and that's important because we all know that fat is flavor. All meat is going to have some fat on top of the cuts, but what you want to look for is good fat content *within* the meat. Pork belly, which has a high fat content within the meat, is a perfect example of this and it's why it's one of the most popular cuts.

COMMON PORK BREEDS

These are the most common breeds of pork sold in the United States. From Yorkshire to Landrace, they all have slightly different characteristics.

Yorkshire Yorkshire pigs are the most popular breed in the United States. They produce large amounts of meat and are typically known for their good bacon and hams.

Duroc Duroc pigs are the second most common breed of pigs in the United States. They are very easy to identify because of their red color. They are known for producing a large amount of lean, high-quality meat.

Berkshire Berkshire pigs are an English breed that are black in color with white tips. They are known for juicy, tender, and flavorful meat that is heavily marbled with fat. They are regarded as the Angus equivalent of pork.

Landrace Landrace pigs are very similar to Yorkshire pigs, but they have droopy ears. They were originally bred to produce long-bodied animals that would produce more bacon per pig. They are now known for their ability to produce lean meat in the hams and loin.

EXOTIC BREEDS

There are a lot of different exotic breeds of pork. Here are a few that I like, from the always delicious Iberico pork all the way to wild boar.

Mangalitsa Mangalitsa pork is a breed indigenous to Hungary. The name means "hog with a lot of lard." It's a breed that has a lot of curly hair, making it look like a sheep. Notably, the breed almost went extinct by the 1990s when there were only 200 pigs remaining in Hungary. Because of the high fat content, the meat can be dried for a longer period of time, which deepens the flavor without losing the moisture. (I had the opportunity to try this amazing meat on my 3-million-subscribers special and the meat was sweet, but also savory. It was some of the best pork I've ever tasted.)

Black Iberian Iberico bellota is one of the finest pork varieties in the world. It comes from free-range pigs that feed mostly on acorns in Spain. This pork variety also produces the "Wagyu version" of pork: Iberico Secreto. This ham is known for its smooth texture, savory taste, and consistent marbling. These legs are some of the most expensive in the world. (I've featured this ham several times on my channel, and it is an experience just to try this meat.)

Warthog Javali, also known as warthog, is found mostly in the African savanna. Its meat has the same flavor and aroma as pork, but it's a lot leaner. Warthogs usually eat grass, fruit, and berries. I had the opportunity to try this in Brazil on my uncle's farm, and it tastes like a cross between pork and beef.

Wild boar Wild boar, though a relative to pigs, does not really taste like pork. It is surprisingly milder than javali and has a slightly darker color, but it still has a nice flavor that is rich and nutty. Wild boars usually feed on nuts, berries, and seeds, but they do occasionally eat meat.

PORK

THE RECIPES

CRISPY & TENDER
PORK PICNIC ROAST

One of the biggest challenges with barbecue is making pork roast that is both crackling and tender. This is because you have to cook it nice and slow to get it tender, but when you do that you can lose the crackling. After lots of experimenting, however, I've finally figured out how to make this almost impossible task possible.

10lb (4.5kg) pork picnic shoulder
1 cup white vinegar
Coarse kosher salt, to taste
Guga's BBQ Rub (p. 200), to taste

TIP *It's extremely important to catch the fat drippings; you do not want to let them drip directly onto the coals, as that can cause a grease fire. If this happens, close all the vents to put out the fire and then start over.*

TIP *If you're cooking with charcoal, you should use lump charcoal for this recipe and not wood.*

PREP AND SEASONING

1 Bring a large pot of water to a boil over medium-high heat. Fill a large bowl with ice water and place a wire rack on a baking tray. Set aside.

2 Pat the pork shoulder dry with paper towels. Using the sharp edge of a boning knife, scrape the skin but do not cut it. (Scraping will help remove extra moisture from the skin.)

3 Using a tenderizing tool or fork, pierce holes in the skin, but be careful not to pierce the meat.

4 Carefully add the pork shoulder to the boiling water. Boil for 10 minutes, and then immediately submerge the shoulder in the ice water for 10 minutes. Remove the shoulder from the ice water, and pat it dry with paper towels. Using the tenderizing tool or fork, poke additional holes in the skin, again being careful not to pierce the meat.

5 Using a basting brush, brush the skin with the white vinegar until the skin is thoroughly coated.

6 Place the shoulder on the prepared rack. Transfer to the fridge to rest, uncovered, for 12 hours. After 12 hours, rinse under cold water to remove the vinegar, and then pat dry with paper towels. Place the shoulder back on the wire rack. Refrigerate, uncovered, for another 12 hours to complete the drying of the skin.

LET'S DO IT!

1 Set up the grill for indirect cooking. Preheat the grill (or smoker) to 300°F (149°C). Place a disposable aluminum foil pan underneath the shoulder to catch the fat drippings. (Do not add water to the pan.)

2 Insert a meat thermometer into the pork shoulder, but don't let it touch the bone. Place the shoulder on the grill or in the smoker. Cook for 6 hours or until the internal temperature reaches 205°F (96°C). (If you're using a drum smoker, there is nothing else to do at this point. If you're using a kettle grill, you will need to rotate the meat every hour to ensure it cooks evenly.) When the internal temperature reaches 205°F (96°C), poke the shoulder with an instant-read thermometer. If it goes into the meat like a hot knife through room-temperature butter, it's ready to be pulled from the smoker or grill.

3 Transfer the shoulder to a cutting board. Use a boning knife to remove the skin and then remove any extra fat from the skin. (The skin should be hard, like crackling.) Add any trimmed fat back to the meat.

4 Wrap the meat and fat in plastic wrap and then aluminum foil. Place in a cold oven or cooler to rest for 1 hour.

5 Once the resting time is complete, place the meat in a large pan and then use two forks to shred. Season to taste with the kosher salt and Guga's BBQ Rub.

6 Serve with the cracklings on the side. (You won't need BBQ sauce, but you are welcome to use it if you like!) The crackling must be eaten right away, but the meat makes great pulled pork sandwiches and can be left in the fridge for up to 5 days.

PORCHETTA

Although this recipe is super easy to make, it should be reserved for special occasions—it's an absolute showstopper! I like to make it for special holiday celebrations. Traditional porchetta is an Italian recipe, but mine is anything but traditional. I guarantee it will taste ten times better than turkey on Thanksgiving!

10lb (4.5kg) pork belly (with loin attached)

2 tbsp olive oil

½ cup diced shallots

¼ cup finely chopped fresh sage

1 tbsp finely chopped fresh rosemary

3 tbsp fresh thyme leaves

Coarse kosher salt

2 tbsp ground black pepper

Zest of 6 lemons

1 cup grated Parmesan cheese

TIP *If the skin did not turn out as crispy as you'd hoped, separate it from the meat and stick it in the microwave on high for 30 to 60 seconds.*

TIP *Add vegetables like carrots and potatoes in the catch tray underneath the porchetta. They will be super flavorful!*

PREP AND SEASONING

1   Pat the pork belly dry with paper towels. Using a filet knife, slice the pork belly on the meat side just enough that it opens into two halves, but do not cut it completely into two separate halves. (Be careful not to pierce the skin as you do this.)

2   Lightly coat the meat side of the pork belly with the olive oil to ensure the seasonings will stick. Spread the shallots, sage, rosemary, thyme leaves, kosher salt, black pepper, lemon zest, and Parmesan over the cut surface.

3   Roll the pork belly up as tightly as possible. Using a trussing needle and butcher's twine, truss the ends and then tightly truss the pork belly at 1½-inch intervals, tying the knots on the bottom side of the porchetta. (The tied pork belly should be able to stand on end without coming undone. There will be a lot of rendered fat during the cooking process, so you want to make sure this beauty is tied up tight!)

4   Using a tenderizing tool or fork, pierce the skin as much as possible, but do not go too deep; you are only trying to pierce small holes to let the rendered fat penetrate the skin. This will help fry the skin.

5   Place a wire rack on a tray and then place the pork belly on the rack. Transfer to the fridge to rest, uncovered, overnight. (There will be some juices dripping, so the tray is a must.)

TIP *Try to find pork belly with the loin still attached. It's a special cut, so you will need to ask your butcher to prepare this for you.*

LET'S DO IT!

1   Set up the grill for indirect heat. Place the porchetta and wire rack on a disposable aluminum catch tray to catch any fat drippings. Preheat to 350°F (177°C).

2   Transfer the porchetta to the grill. Insert a meat thermometer into the porchetta.

3   Once the internal temperature reaches 175°F (79°C), remove the porchetta from the grill and discard the drip tray. Bring the grill heat up as high as possible, ideally between 600°F and 700°F (316°C and 371°C) to get a good crackling. (You can also use your oven broiler to achieve this.)

4   Return the porchetta to the grill. (You'll want to watch the porchetta like a hawk at this stage! It can take anywhere from 3 to 10 minutes to get the skin to puff up and turn golden-brown, and that's what you want. If it gets too dark, remove it from the heat immediately.)

5   Let the porchetta rest, uncovered, for at least 30 minutes so the juices can redistribute and the crackling can become even better. Slice before serving.

HOT & FAST
ST. LOUIS–STYLE RIBS

There are many types of ribs—baby back ribs, loin ribs, and so many others—and this recipe will work for any of them. But honestly, spare ribs are the best of the best. Once you master how to cook perfect ribs, everything else will be so easy!

2 full racks St. Louis–style ribs

Coarse kosher salt

Guga's BBQ Rub (p. 200)

1 cup Guga's BBQ Sauce (p. 201)

PREP AND SEASONING

1   Using a butter knife, loosen a corner of the membrane from the back of the ribs. Once you've lifted a small corner of the membrane, grasp the corner with a paper towel and pull the membrane away to remove it. Repeat with the second rack.

2   Liberally season all sides of the racks with kosher salt followed by a liberal dusting of Guga's BBQ Rub.

TIP *Many people like to use a binder to help the seasonings stick to the ribs. I don't think it's necessary, but if you find the seasonings aren't sticking to the meat, just lightly coat the ribs with some grapeseed oil and then apply the salt and rub.*

LET'S DO IT!

1   Preheat the smoker to 250°F (121°C).

2   Place the ribs in the smoker. Let them cook for about 4 hours or until the internal temperature reaches 175°F (79°C). The goal is to get nice color on the ribs and also develop a deep smoky flavor.

3   After 4 hours, remove the ribs from the smoker and tightly wrap them in butcher paper. Place them back in the smoker and continue smoking until they reach an internal temperature of 203°F (95°C), about 30 minutes.

4   Once the correct temperature is reached, take the ribs out of the smoker, remove and discard the butcher's paper, and brush all sides of the ribs with the Guga's BBQ Sauce. Place the ribs back in the smoker for another 30 minutes to finish them off.

5   Allow the ribs to rest for at least 30 minutes and up to 1 hour before cutting into individual ribs and serving.

DO IT LIKE GUGA!

Dry brining the ribs overnight will make them taste even better! Also, cooking these ribs the night before serving is highly recommended. Simply wrap them in butcher paper and stick them in an oven at 150°F (66°C) for at least 6 hours or, better yet, overnight. Trust me: the longer they rest, the better they will taste!

SMOKED BABY BACK RIBS

Baby backs are the most popular style of pork ribs, and they have much more meat than other styles of pork ribs. These are the only ribs I like falling off the bone. Some might consider that overcooked, but I just love the soft texture and fattiness that comes from cooking them until they're extremely tender.

4 full racks baby back ribs

3 tbsp Worcestershire sauce

Coarse kosher salt

1 cup Guga's BBQ Rub (salt-free version, see tip on page 200)

8 tbsp unsalted butter, divided

1 cup apple juice, divided

1 cup Guga's BBQ Sauce (p. 201)

FOR THE BASTING SPRAY

½ cup red wine vinegar

2 cups water

TIP *If you choose to season and prep the ribs the night before cooking, be sure to wrap the seasoned ribs in plastic wrap so they don't dry out.*

TIP *If you're making the ribs in advance for a party, you can keep the uncut ribs warm in the oven for up to 3 hours by using the Warm setting or placing them in the warming drawer. Just be sure to cover them with aluminum foil so they don't dry out.*

PREP AND SEASONING

1 Combine the red wine vinegar and water in a spray bottle. Set aside.

2 Remove the membrane from the backs of the racks by inserting the handle of a spoon underneath the membrane and in the middle of the ribs. Pull the spoon upward to pull the membrane away from the ribs.

3 Lightly brush both sides of the ribs with the Worcestershire sauce. (This will create a binder for the seasonings.)

4 Liberally season only the top sides with kosher salt and then season both sides with the salt-free version of the Guga's BBQ Rub.

5 Place the ribs on sheet pans, and then transfer them to the fridge to rest while you prepare the smoker.

LET'S DO IT!

1 Preheat the smoker to 225°F (107°C).

2 Place the ribs in the smoker. Smoke for 3 hours, spraying the ribs every 30 minutes with the vinegar-water solution to ensure the bark remains soft. (Check the ribs occasionally and keep an eye on the color. If they are becoming too dark, smoke them for less time; if they are too light, continue smoking for the full amount of time.)

3 While the ribs are smoking, cut 2 large sheets of aluminum foil and then turn the edges up slightly to form "trays." Into the center of each tray, add 4 tablespoons of the butter and ½ cup apple juice.

4 After 3 hours, remove the ribs from the smoker. Place two racks in each foil tray. Wrap them as tightly as possible in the foil.

5 Place the wrapped ribs back in the smoker and cook for 1 to 2 hours more or until the internal temperature reaches 203°F (95°C) on a meat thermometer and the thermometer inserts easily into the ribs like a knife going through room-temperature butter. (Some racks may cook more quickly than others, so be on the lookout and pull them earlier, if needed.)

6 Once the ribs are fully cooked, remove them from the smoker. Remove and discard the foil. (You can collect the juices from the foil and save them for use as a basting liquid for your next ribs cook.)

7 Lightly brush the ribs with Guga's BBQ Sauce. (Don't overdo the sauce. You just want a nice glaze on the ribs. You can always add more later.)

8 Place the ribs back in the smoker. Cook just until the sauce sets and is no longer dripping, about 5 to 10 minutes. (Do not leave them in for too long! BBQ sauce has lots of sugar, which can burn quickly.)

9 Remove the ribs from the smoker, and let them rest for 10 to 20 minutes before cutting and serving.

TENDER & JUICY
PORK LOIN

This pork loin is so incredibly delicious! It's the perfect weekday dinner; it's easy to make, inexpensive, and most importantly, it takes almost no time at all to prepare.
I cook this often and even my kids love it! It's so tender, you won't even need teeth to chew it! Ha!

3lb (1.36kg) pork loin
Coarse kosher salt
8 tbsp butter

FOR THE RUB
1 tbsp ground black pepper
1 tbsp granulated garlic
1 tbsp smoked paprika
1 tbsp granulated onion

TIP *For an even more tender result and deeper seasoning, try dry brining the pork loin overnight.*

TIP *You can triple the rub ingredients and store the remaining rub for future use. It's equally great on pork, chicken, and fish!*

PREP AND SEASONING

1   Pat the pork loin dry with paper towels. Using a filet knife, lift and peel away any silver skin from the pork loin.

2   Make the rub by combining the black pepper, granulated garlic, smoked paprika, and granulated onion in a small bowl. Set aside.

3   Liberally season the pork loin with kosher salt, making sure to evenly coat all sides.

4   Lightly sprinkle the rub over the pork loin, making sure to evenly coat all sides.

5   Melt the butter in a small dish in the microwave. Now get your basting brush ready; it's time to grill!

LET'S DO IT!

1   Set up the grill for two-zone cooking. Preheat to 350°F (177°C).

2   Place the pork loin over direct heat. Sear on all sides, turning frequently, until it's browned on all sides, about 2 minutes.

3   Move the loin to indirect heat. Cook for 1 minute, basting continuously, and then move the loin back to the direct heat. Sear for 2 minutes more, turning the loin frequently to ensure the flames do not touch any one side for any longer than 10 to 15 seconds.

4   Move the pork loin back to indirect heat. Baste again with the butter, and then continue cooking over indirect heat, turning the loin frequently, until it reaches an internal temperature of 145°F (63°C).

5   Remove the pork loin from the grill. Set it aside to rest for 5 minutes before slicing and serving.

DO IT LIKE GUGA!

This pork loin is delicious served with some steamed rice and sliced tomatoes that have been drizzled with olive oil and then seasoned with salt, black pepper, and a pinch of dried oregano.

IBERICO SECRETO
(THE WAGYU OF PORK)

This one is something truly special! I still remember the first time I tried it. Even though it's pork, it does not taste like pork; it's more similar to steak, but it's very fatty and has a rich, buttery, sweet-and-savory flavor that can't be explained. You have to try it! You are about to cook something you will never forget!

2lb (907g) iberico secreto

Coarse kosher salt

Ground black pepper

Granulated garlic

TIP *This meat is expensive and nearly impossible to find in a regular supermarket, so ordering it online is the easiest way to get it.*

PREP AND SEASONING

1   Pat the iberico secreto dry with paper towels. If there is an excessive amount of external fat, use a sharp knife to trim some of it. (Don't trim all of it; you want to leave some intact.)

2   Season the iberico secreto lightly with kosher salt, black pepper, and granulated garlic.

TIP *This cut is truly something special, so you don't want to mask the flavor by adding any overpowering rubs or other strong seasonings. Just keep it simple and the meat will shine.*

LET'S DO IT!

1   Set up the grill for two-zone cooking. Preheat to 350°F (177°C).

2   Place the iberico secreto over the direct heat. After about 30 seconds, the meat will begin to flare up like there is no tomorrow. Once this happens, use tongs to immediately move the meat to the indirect side until the flames subside.

3   Flip the iberico secreto and repeat the process, doing all you can to prevent the flare-ups from touching the meat.

4   Continue moving the meat to and from the direct heat and flipping it until you get a beautiful golden-brown crust. (With this cut, the internal temperature is not as important as the crust, but I try to keep the final cooking temperature between 140°F and 145°F [60°C and 63°C]. What I really try to focus on more is developing that beautiful golden-brown crust.)

5   Once the crust is perfect, remove the meat from the grill and let it rest for 5 minutes before cutting it against the grain and into thin strips. Serve warm.

DO IT LIKE GUGA!

It's all about the grill setup for this one, so if you're cooking with charcoal, make sure you don't add too much charcoal to the grill. Also, be sure to keep some distance between the grill grate and the charcoal. The key is to keep moving this amazing piece of meat on and off the direct heat to minimize flare-ups and to prevent burning the crust. It's a difficult cut to grill since it has so much fat, but don't let that stop you! This one is truly an experience!

SMOKED HONEY HAM

If you want to impress your guests over the holidays, this is the recipe that will do it. The amount of effort required to put this recipe together is minimal, so there's no excuse not to make it! It's so good, it just might outshine your turkey this holiday season!

5–8lb (2.25–3.60kg) fully cooked ham

¼ cup whole cloves (optional)

5 tbsp brown sugar

10 pineapple slices (optional)

FOR THE HONEY GLAZE

5 tbsp maple syrup

5 tbsp honey

10 tbsp brown sugar

2 tbsp bourbon (alternatively, use 2 tbsp butter)

2 tbsp water

PREP AND SEASONING

1   Pat the ham dry with paper towels. Using a sharp knife, lightly score the surface of the ham in a crisscross pattern. (Don't score the ham too deep; you just want to score it to about a ¼-inch [0.65cm] depth.)

2   Press the cloves (if using) into the areas where the meat has been scored. Set aside.

3   Make the honey glaze by combining the glaze ingredients in a nonstick saucepan over medium-low heat. Stir continuously until the brown sugar is melted. Set aside.

LET'S DO IT!

1   Preheat the smoker to 250°F (121°C). Place a foil-lined drip pan underneath the area where the ham will be cooking. (This will make cleanup much easier.)

2   Place the ham in the smoker. Smoke for 25 minutes, and then remove the ham from the smoker.

3   Pat the brown sugar over the entire scored surface of the ham, and then arrange the pineapple slices (if using) over the scored surface of the ham. Place the ham back in the smoker for 10 minutes to allow the sugars to crystalize.

4   After 10 minutes, open the smoker and brush the honey glaze over the entire surface of the ham. Repeat the glazing every 10 minutes until the ham is nicely glazed and the internal temperature reaches 165°F (74°C), about 1½ to 2 hours. (Don't let the glaze get too dark or it will become bitter. If the internal temperature has not been reached but the color on the exterior of the ham is good, you can take the ham out of the smoker since it's already fully cooked.)

5   Remove the ham from the smoker, and let it rest for 10 to 15 minutes before slicing and serving.

DO IT LIKE GUGA!

Be patient with the glazing process! The more you do it, the better it will be. I usually glaze the ham for the first hour of cooking, which makes the glaze nice and crunchy. (The crunchy glaze is my family's favorite part!)

SWEET & SPICY
PORK BELLY

If you love pork, you know the best part of the hog is the belly! The belly also happens to be the part that bacon is made from. (The saying "Bacon makes everything better" is so true.) When you combine pork belly with sweet and spicy flavors, you'll take your barbecue to another level!

4lb (1.80kg) skin-on pork belly
Coarse kosher salt
Ground back pepper
Fine table salt

FOR THE SWEET-AND-SPICY SAUCE

6 tbsp guava paste
1–2 tbsp sriracha sauce
1 tbsp water

TIP *If you prefer the sauce be more sweet than spicy, reduce the amount of sriracha. You can also replace the guava paste with equal amounts of plum paste or even strawberry jelly, but I much prefer the guava paste.*

TIP *Lots of fat will be rendered from the pork belly, so it's extremely important that you have something to catch that fat. If the fat touches the fire, you could end up with a grease fire. If that happens, you'll need to cut off all oxygen to the fire and start over.*

PREP AND SEASONING

1   Make the sweet-and-spicy sauce by combining the guava paste, 1 to 2 tablespoons sriracha sauce (adjust the amount based on how spicy you prefer the sauce to be), and the water in a blender or food processor. Blend until smooth. (If needed, add additional water in small amounts until the sauce is nice and smooth, but not runny.) Set aside.

2   Pat the pork belly dry with paper towels. Using a sharp knife, scrape the skin to remove as much moisture as possible. (The more you scrape, the more moisture the skin will release.) Pat the skin dry again with clean paper towels.

3   Transfer the pork belly to a large tray. Place it in the fridge, uncovered, to dry out overnight.

4   After the drying time is complete, use a sharp knife to score the skin in a crisscross pattern. Be sure to only score the skin; you don't want to penetrate the fat. (This step will prevent the pork belly from curling up as it cooks.)

5   Liberally season only the meat side with kosher salt and black pepper.

6   Place the pork belly on a cooling rack that is sitting on top of a baking tray. Now let's get cooking!

LET'S DO IT!

1   Set up the grill for indirect cooking. Preheat to 375°F (191°C).

2   Spread a generous, even layer of fine table salt over the entire surface of the skin. (This will allow the skin to dry out and crisp up even more. As the fat is rendering, the salt will absorb the fat to create a layer of salt that you can then peel off.)

3   Place the pork belly skin-side up on the cooling rack and baking tray over indirect heat. Cook until the internal temperature reaches 170°F (77°C), about 2 to 3 hours. Once the pork belly reaches temperature, remove it from the grill and then remove and discard the salt layer.

4   Open the air vents (if you're cooking on a charcoal grill) or turn the burners on the direct side up to high (if you're cooking on a gas grill). You want the grill to get hot! (Keep in mind you will still be cooking indirectly; you just want the grill to be hot!)

5   Place the pork belly skin-side up on the cooling rack and baking tray and then place it back over indirect heat. Cook for an additional 5 to 10 minutes to crisp the skin. (You will need to watch it like a hawk! You'll want to open the lid every minute to check the skin. If the skin gets too dark, remove the pork belly from the grill. You just want to create blisters on the skin. Alternatively, you can crisp the skin under the oven broiler for 30 seconds to 1 minute.)

6   Once the skin is nice and crispy, transfer the pork belly to a cutting board. Slice it into 1-inch x 1-inch (2.5cm x 2.5cm) cubes, and then transfer the cubes to a large bowl. Drizzle a generous amount of the sweet-and-spicy sauce over the top of the pork belly pieces, and then toss to coat. Allow to rest for 20 to 45 minutes before serving.

BBQ PULLED PORK

This recipe takes some serious time and patience to make, but it will make you the talk of the neighborhood BBQ community! It's the perfect summer barbecue dish and will have everyone asking for the recipe. It works great for sandwiches, but you can also pair it with potato salad or just enjoy it all by itself. This pulled pork is absolutely amazing!

8–12lb (3.65–5.45kg) skinless pork shoulder

Guga's BBQ Rub (p. 200)

Guga's BBQ Sauce (p. 201)

FOR THE MARINADE

Juice of 4 medium sour oranges (or the juice of 4 navel oranges and 2 limes)

½ cup water

½ cup white wine

10 garlic cloves

Juice of 4 medium limes

4 tbsp soy sauce

4 tbsp smoked paprika

4 tbsp apple cider vinegar

4 tbsp olive oil

3 tbsp coarse kosher salt

PREP AND SEASONING

1 Using a sharp paring knife, poke holes over the entire surface of the pork shoulder. Set aside.

2 Make the marinade by combining all the ingredients in a blender. Blend until well combined and smooth.

3 Using a marinade injector, inject some of the marinade into the pork shoulder.

4 Place the pork shoulder in a vacuum bag or large freezer bag, and then pour the remaining marinade into the bag. Seal and then place the bag in a second vacuum bag or large freezer bag to prevent leakage. Place the pork shoulder in the fridge to marinate for 24 hours.

5 Once the marinating time is complete, remove the pork shoulder from the bags and discard the marinade. Use paper towels to pat the pork shoulder dry. Use a sharp paring knife to poke small holes in the surface to release the moisture.

LET'S DO IT!

1 Preheat the smoker to 275°F (135°C).

2 Place the pork shoulder in the smoker. Smoke for 3 to 4 hours, and then remove it from the smoker and wrap it tightly in aluminum foil.

3 Place it back in the smoker. Continue smoking until it reaches an internal temperature of 200°F (93°C) to 205°F (96°C), about 3 to 4 hours.

4 Once the pork shoulder reaches the proper temperature, transfer it to large cooler or an oven set to the lowest setting. Let it rest for at least 12 hours or overnight.

5 After the resting time is complete, transfer the pork shoulder to a cutting board. Use two forks to shred.

6 Season liberally with Guga's BBQ Rub, and then add as much Guga's BBQ Sauce as you desire. Toss the shredded pork in the sauce to coat. Serve warm.

CHAR SIU BBQ PORK

I always loved eating this pork at Chinese restaurants, but then I found out how easy it was to make it at home, so I've been making it myself ever since. This is one of my favorite dishes to make, and I just know that once you try this, it will be one of your favorites too!

8–12lb (3.65–5.45kg) pork shoulder, deboned and cut into 2-inch-thick (5cm thick) slices

FOR THE MARINADE

9 garlic cloves, minced

9 tbsp brown sugar

9 tbsp honey

3 tsp Chinese five spice blend

6 tbsp cherry vinegar (or apple cider vinegar)

3 tbsp dark soy sauce

6 tbsp hoisin sauce

9 tsp sesame oil

15 cubes Chinese fermented red bean curd

Coarse kosher salt, to taste

TIP *Fermented Chinese red bean curd is commonly sold in jars at most Asian groceries.*

PREP AND SEASONING

1   Combine the garlic, brown sugar, honey, Chinese five spice blend, cherry vinegar, dark soy sauce, hoisin sauce, sesame oil, and fermented bean curd in a large saucepan over medium-low heat. Stir to combine.

2   Bring the ingredients to a boil, and then turn off the heat. (The sauce is done once it reaches a boil.) Season to taste with kosher salt.

3   Place the pork slices in a large bowl.

4   Transfer half the marinade to an airtight container. Place in the fridge until you're ready to cook. Add the remaining marinade to the bowl with the pork slices. Toss to coat.

5   Cover the bowl with plastic wrap, and then place the pork in the fridge to marinate for 8 hours or overnight. (Alternatively, place the coated pork in a vacuum bag, seal, and place it in the fridge to marinate. The vacuum seal will help the marinade penetrate even deeper into the meat.)

TIP *If you want the color of the pork to be bright red like it often appears when you order it for takeout, add a few drops of red food coloring to the sauce. (This will do nothing to affect the flavor, but it will enhance the color.)*

LET'S DO IT!

1   Preheat the smoker to 250°F (121°C).

2   Place the pork strips directly on the smoker grates. Smoke for 1 to 2 hours, occasionally spooning the sauce over the meat to prevent it from drying out. (The meat should always look moist.) Smoke until the meat reaches an internal temperature of 165°F (74°C).

3   Remove the pork slices from the smoker and place in a large pan. Cover with aluminum foil and place in a food warmer, or oven on the lowest setting, to rest for at least 1 hour. Serve warm.

DO IT LIKE GUGA!

It's very important to cook this pork low and slow, so watch your smoker temperature carefully. The brown sugar in the marinade can burn and become bitter if the smoker temperature is too high.

BURGERS, TACOS, SANDWICHES & MORE

BIRRIA TACOS

These tacos are one of the greatest gifts given to humankind. Now, I know that's a big statement, but it's for good reason: these tacos seem to have come from the heavens!

10lb (4.54kg) beef short ribs, trimmed

8¼ cups (2L) water

30 small corn tortillas

3lb (1.35kg) shredded mozzarella cheese

Coarse kosher salt

For the adobo marinade

20 garlic cloves

1 tbsp ginger paste

2 tbsp olive oil, divided

1 large sweet onion, diced

2lb (907g) small red tomatoes, quartered

5 dried chile ancho

5 dried chile guajillo

5 dried chile puya

1 tbsp allspice berries

1 tbsp ground black pepper

1 tbsp cumin

1 tbsp dried oregano

½ cinnamon stick

3 tbsp coarse kosher salt

¼ cup apple cider vinegar

For serving

1 cup finely diced white onion

1 cup finely chopped fresh cilantro

Birria Tacos Red Sauce (p. 206)

Birria Tacos Green Sauce (p. 207)

PREP AND SEASONING

1   Begin making the marinade by using a mortar and pestle to pound the garlic cloves and ginger into a paste. Set aside.

2   In a medium sauté pan over medium heat, heat 1 tablespoon olive oil. Add the onion. Cook until lightly browned, and then add the tomatoes.

3   While the tomatoes are cooking, heat the remaining 1 tablespoon olive oil in a separate medium sauté pan over medium heat. Add the ancho, guajillo, and puya chiles. Sauté for 2 minutes or until the color starts to change slightly. (If needed, add 1 to 2 tablespoons water to rehydrate the chiles.)

4   Add the garlic-ginger paste to the pan with the chiles. Stir and then add the allspice berries, black pepper, cumin, dried oregano, cinnamon stick, kosher salt, and vinegar. Cook for 2 minutes.

5   Combine the ingredients from both pans in a blender. Blend until a smooth paste is formed. Set aside.

6   In a large stock pot over high heat, add the short ribs, adobo marinade, and water. Bring to a boil. Once boiling, reduce the heat to medium and bring to a low, rolling boil. Cover and cook for 5 to 6 hours. The short ribs are done when they're falling off the bone. Transfer the cooked short ribs to a separate container, and pull the meat from the bones. Place the meat in a resealable container and discard the bones. Cover and place it in the fridge. Strain the broth into a resealable container. Cover and place in the fridge overnight.

7   Remove the meat and broth from the fridge. Use a spoon to remove the adobo fat to a separate container.

LET'S DO IT!

1   Add the broth to a large pot over medium-low heat.

2   Place a large flat-top griddle on the stove top over medium-low heat. Place a large cast-iron skillet on top of the flat-top griddle or over medium heat. Add the reserved adobo fat to the skillet. Let it melt.

3   Dunk the tortillas into the melted fat and then place them on the flat-top griddle to fry. Transfer the fried tortillas to a serving platter.

4   Place the short rib meat in the cast-iron skillet. Heat until the meat is warmed through.

5   Sprinkle a generous amount of cheese on top of a tortilla and then place a generous portion of meat on one half of the tortilla. Use a spatula to close the tortilla. Repeat with the remaining tortillas.

6   Spoon a generous amount of the adobo fat on top of the tacos. (This will help make the tortillas crispy and also change the color to red.)

7   Open the tacos and top with a generous pinch of diced onion and a generous pinch of chopped cilantro. Drizzle the red taco sauce and green taco sauce over the top.

8   Pour 1 cup of the broth into a cup and serve on the side.

SMASH BURGER
(THE BURGER THAT CHANGED MY LIFE)

When I say this burger changed my life, I mean it! I used to think a good burger always had to be fat and juicy, but boy, was I wrong! The secret to this burger is the Maillard reaction combined with using good ground beef and just cheap American cheese. All you need to take this burger to the next level is Guga's Burger Buns and Guga's Basic Burger Sauce!

3lb (1.35kg) ground beef (80/20 blend)

8 Guga's Burger Buns (p. 145) or brioche buns

4 tbsp butter

½ cup Guga's Basic Burger Sauce (p. 214)

1 tbsp grapeseed oil

Coarse kosher salt

Ground black pepper

16 slices processed American cheese (I like Kraft brand)

PREP AND SEASONING

1   Shape the ground beef into 16 equal-sized balls (3oz/85g each). Place the balls on a platter and set aside. (Making the balls the same size ensures they will make great-looking burgers.)

2   Get your tools and supplies ready. You'll need protective gloves, a burger smasher or spatula, a cast-iron griddle or skillet, a lid for covering the burgers, parchment paper cut into 16 burger-sized squares, and a burger scraper. This is live action cooking, so let's go! It's time to shine!

TIP   *Be sure to use protective gloves as your hands will get close to the fire and fat splattering is inevitable. Be sure to have everything ready to go before you begin cooking so you can move quickly and make a burger every 1 to 2 minutes. (This is so much fun!)*

LET'S DO IT!

1   Set up your grill for direct cooking. Preheat to 400°F (204°C).

2   Split the buns and spread some butter over the split sides of each bun. Toast the buns briefly on the grill, and then spread 1 tablespoon of the burger sauce on the bottom bun. Set aside.

3   Place the cast-iron griddle or skillet on the grill grate. (You want the griddle or skillet to be super hot, but not so hot that it burns the seasoning from the surface.)

4   Add the grapeseed oil to the griddle or skillet, and then place two burger balls on the hot griddle or skillet. Place a piece of parchment paper on top of each ball to prevent the burgers from sticking to the burger smasher. Using your burger smasher or a spatula, smash the balls as thin as you can without breaking them apart.

5   Remove the parchment paper and then lightly season the top sides of the burgers with kosher salt and black pepper. Once the juices start flowing, immediately use the burger scraper to flip the burger. (You want to really scrape the burger from the surface to ensure you get the crust! The juices will start flowing within 30 seconds to 1 minute, depending on how thin you've smashed the patties.)

6   Immediately place 1 slice of the cheese on top of each burger and then cover the grill with the lid for about 30 seconds or just until the cheese is melted. (If you cook these burgers on a stove top, you can use a sheet pan or anything else that won't attach to the cheese, but will still trap the steam to melt the cheese.)

7   Using the scraper, scrape one patty and carefully place it on top of the second patty, then scrape both patties out of the griddle or skillet and place them on the bottom bun.

8   Top the smash burger with the top bun. Serve immediately and then make hundreds more! It's the best of the best!

SMOKED BURGER
WITH RED CHIMICHURRI SAUCE

Sometimes you're just in the mood for a fat, juicy burger. When that craving hits, this is the one to make. It's not like just any traditional burger, it's smoky and flavorful.

3lb (1.35kg) ground beef (80/20 blend)

2lb (907g) ground pork

½ cup seasoned bread crumbs

½ cup finely chopped white onion

4 garlic cloves, minced

3 egg yolks

1 tbsp coarse kosher salt

½ tbsp ground black pepper

1 tbsp dried parsley

½ tbsp dried oregano

½ tbsp granulated garlic

10 Guga's Burger Buns (p. 145) or plain burger buns

10 tbsp butter

20 slices provolone cheese

FOR TOPPING

Guga's Spicy Burger Sauce (p. 214)

Red Chimichurri Sauce (p. 211)

10 crisp iceberg lettuce leaves (optional)

2 large red tomatoes, sliced (optional)

1 large white onion, sliced (optional)

20–30 dill pickle slices (optional)

PREP AND SEASONING

1 Combine the ground beef, ground pork, bread crumbs, onion, garlic, egg yolks, kosher salt, black pepper, dried parsley, dried oregano, and granulated garlic in a large bowl. Mix until well combined.

2 Split the buns. Set aside.

3 Shape the burger mixture into 10 large, fat patties that are approximately 8 ounces (227g) each. (Make the burgers tight enough that they will keep their shapes during cooking, but not too tight. You still want them to have the texture of a burger.) Place the burgers on a cooling rack and get the smoker ready.

TIP *This is supposed to be a fat, juicy burger, so you don't want flat patties. You will lose 15 to 20 percent of the fat in the cooking process, so they will shrink. Try to make them slightly larger and thicker than the buns.*

LET'S DO IT!

1 Preheat the smoker to 285°F (141°C). Preheat the grill to low.

2 Transfer the burgers and cooling rack to the smoker. Smoke the burgers for 30 to 45 minutes or until the internal temperature reaches 160°F (71°C).

3 While the burgers are smoking, spread 1 tablespoon butter over the split sides of each bun. Add as much Guga's Spicy Burger Sauce as you prefer.

4 Increase the grill heat to high. Once the grill is hot and the burgers have reached the desired temperature, place them on the hot grill to add a quick sear. (You can also use a flamethrower, which will make quick work of the searing.)

5 Place 2 slices of provolone on the burger patty. Allow the cheese to melt, but don't let it burn. (If you're using a flamethrower to melt the cheese, watch it carefully. You can also use your oven broiler to melt the cheese.)

6 Place the burgers on the buns and then top with the Red Chimichurri Sauce. If desired, add a lettuce leaf, a few tomato slices, a few onion slices, and a few pickle slices. You are ready to go!

DO IT LIKE GUGA!

If you don't have a smoker, a charcoal grill, and a flamethrower, get them! They are amazing cooking tools. With that being said, you can also make this recipe indoors by searing the burgers in a cast-iron skillet and then broiling them in the oven.

DEEP-FRIED BURGER

This is an amazing burger! It's inexpensive and easy to make, and it gets better and better the more you make because the seasoned oil gets more flavorful as you cook more burgers. This is why Dyer's Burgers in Memphis, Tennessee, has been doing this to perfection for decades. Now, to be honest, my version is a little different and a little easier to make, as no one has access to the decades-old oil from Dyer's!

3lb (1.35kg) ground beef (80/20 blend)

8 Guga's Burger Buns (p. 145) or brioche buns

½ cup Guga's Basic Burger Sauce (p. 214)

16 slices processed American cheese (I like Kraft brand)

FOR THE SEASONED FRYING OIL

42fl oz (1.25L) Wagyu beef tallow

30 garlic cloves

Handful of fresh thyme

10 tbsp Worcestershire sauce

5 tbsp soy sauce

1 tsp Liquid Smoke

PREP AND SEASONING

1   Form the ground beef into 16 (3oz/85g) balls. Place the balls on a platter and transfer to the fridge.

2   Prepare the seasoned frying oil by placing all of the ingredients in a cast-iron pan over medium-low heat. Simmer for 30 to 45 minutes or until the oil becomes fragrant. (Watch the oil closely. If the garlic begins to get too dark, remove it from the pan. It's all about the garlic!) Remove the oil from the heat and then strain into a heatproof container.

3   Get your equipment and supplies ready! You'll need a burger smasher or spatula, parchment paper cut into 16 burger-sized squares, a cutting board, burger scraper, and metal fish spatula. It's time to rock!

TIP *If you have the time, there's a slower method for making the seasoned oil that will result in an even more flavorful oil. Place all of the ingredients in the cast-iron skillet and place it in the oven at 275°F (135°C) for 5 to 8 hours, checking it every hour to ensure the garlic is not burning. Strain.*

LET'S DO IT!

1   Add the seasoning oil to a fryer or deep skillet. Preheat to 350°F (177°C).

2   Split and toast the buns. Add 1 tablespoon of the burger sauce to the bottom half of each bun. Set aside.

3   Place a burger ball on the cutting board and then place a piece of parchment paper on top of the ball. Use the burger smasher or spatula to smash the ball into a thin patty. Use the scraper to scrape it off the board and then carefully drop it into the hot oil. Fry until the burger forms a perfect crust, about 2 to 3 minutes depending on how thin the patty is.

4   Use the fish spatula to transfer the patty from the oil to a plate. Place one slice of cheese on top of the first patty.

5   Follow the same steps to cook a second patty. Place the second fried patty on top of the first patty, and then top the second patty with another slice of cheese.

6   Using a large spoon, carefully spoon some of the seasoned oil over the cheese and patties. As the cheese starts to melt, immediately place the patties on a bottom bun and then crown with a top bun. Repeat with the remaining patties. Serve hot.

CLASSIC STEAK SANDWICH

There's nothing better than the perfect steak sandwich. This one is quick and easy to make, and almost foolproof! It's all about the bread and meat with this one, so get those two things right and you will have great success.

16oz (454g) ribeye or New York strip steak (use prime grade, if possible)

Coarse kosher salt

Ground black pepper

Granulated garlic

4 slices artisan sandwich bread (or whatever high-quality bread you prefer)

FOR THE SAUCE

3 tbsp mayonnaise (or an equal amount of Greek yogurt or cream cheese)

1 tbsp prepared horseradish

1 tsp lemon juice

1 tbsp old-style mustard (optional)

Coarse kosher salt and ground black pepper, to taste

FOR THE GARLIC BUTTER

4 tbsp butter

1 tbsp garlic paste

1 tsp chopped fresh parsley

PREP AND SEASONING

1   Pat the steak dry with paper towels. Liberally season with kosher salt, black pepper, and granulated garlic. Set aside.

2   Make the sauce by combining the mayonnaise, horseradish, lemon juice, and mustard (if using) in a small bowl. Mix well. Cover and transfer to the fridge.

3   Make the garlic butter by combining the butter, garlic paste, and chopped parsley in a small bowl. Mix to combine. Set aside.

LET'S DO IT!

1   Set up the grill for two-zone cooking. Preheat to 350°F (177°C).

2   Sear the steak on both sides over direct heat, and then move the steak to indirect heat. Cook until the internal temperature reaches 130°F (54°F). Transfer the steak to a cutting board to rest for 5 to 10 minutes.

3   Split the buns and then spread 1 tablespoon garlic butter over the split sides of each bun. Place the buns split sides down over direct heat to toast briefly. (Be very careful to not let them burn.)

4   Slice the rested steak thinly.

5   Add the sauce to both split sides of the buns. Place the steak on the bottom bun, and then top with the crown. Serve with a cold beer or my favorite: Guaraná Antarctica (a Brazilian soft drink).

DO IT LIKE GUGA!

You can go crazy here! Add cheese, caramelized onions, and charred bell peppers. Make this sandwich your own!

GREEK GYRO

Everybody loves street food, and I'm no different. And while some street foods aren't worth making at home, this one absolutely is! And since you can prepare everything days in advance, there is no reason to not give it a try! Let's do it!

1 medium white onion, quartered

2lb (907g) ground beef (80/20 blend)

1½lb (680g) chopped lamb

2 tbsp garlic powder

2 tbsp coarse kosher salt

2 tbsp dried oregano

2 tbsp ground black pepper

1 tbsp smoked paprika

1 tbsp granulated onion

1 tbsp za'atar seasoning

FOR THE SKEWER

½ large white onion

Large pineapple, halved widthwise

FOR SERVING

4 medium pita breads

1 cup tzatziki sauce

½ large head iceberg lettuce, thinly sliced

½ large onion (purple or white), thinly sliced

3 large red tomatoes, sliced

PREP AND SEASONING

1   Add the onion to a food processor. Pulse until finely chopped.

2   Add the ground beef, chopped lamb, garlic powder, kosher salt, oregano, black pepper, smoked paprika, granulated onion, and za'atar seasoning to the food processor. Process until a smooth paste is formed.

3   Shape the paste into a long, wide log. Insert a skewer lengthwise through the meat so that there are a few inches of the skewer visible on each end. Place the meat on a large sheet of plastic wrap, and roll it up as tightly as possible. Transfer to the fridge to rest overnight.

TIP   *This can also be made on the grill. Set up the grill for indirect cooking and preheat to 400°F (204°C). Place the meat flat on the grill surface. Cook for 35 to 45 minutes, rotating the meat frequently, until the internal temperature reaches 160°F (71°C). (The meat on the outer edges will cook more quickly, so you can shave off the fully cooked meat as it reaches temperature.)*

LET'S DO IT!

1   Remove the middle and top racks in the oven. Preheat the oven to 400°F (204°C).

2   Place the halved onion cut side down in a large cast-iron skillet. Insert one end of the skewered meat into the middle of the onion so that the meat is standing upright. Skewer the halved pineapple on the top end of the skewer and on top of the meat.

3   Place the meat upright in the oven. Cook for 35 to 45 minutes or until the meat reaches an internal temperature of 160°F (71°C), occasionally basting the meat with the pan drippings.

4   Once the edges of the meat begin to char, you can begin shaving pieces away with a sharp knife. (These fully cooked pieces can be enjoyed right away.)

5   To serve, place the pitas on a flat surface. Top with a generous porton of the shaved meat and then drizzle some of the tzatziki sauce over the meat. Top with the lettuce, onion, and tomatoes. Wrap the pita around the fillings and serve. (If desired, you can dice the cooked pineapple and use it as another topping.)

DO IT LIKE GUGA!

If you like to be prepared like I do, you can prep everything a day ahead of your cook. To speed up the process, I like to sous vide the meat at 150°F (66°C) for 3½ hours. All I then have to do is sear the meat in a hot skillet when it's time to eat!

STEAKHOUSE CAST-IRON SKILLET BURGER

This is the perfect burger for any occasion! You can make this one on the grill or indoors. The combination of the sear from the skillet and the basting with the garlic-thyme butter makes this recipe a guaranteed hit every time you make it!

1½lb (680g) ground beef (80/20 blend)

2 brioche buns

Coarse kosher salt

Ground black pepper

6 tbsp butter, divided

2 garlic cloves, divided

2 sprigs fresh thyme, divided

4 slices provolone cheese

Guga's Basic Burger Sauce (p. 214)

PREP AND SEASONING

1 Divide the ground beef into 4 (6oz/170g) balls. Set aside.

2 Split the buns. Set aside.

3 Get your equipment ready. You'll need a large cast-iron skillet, a burger scraper, a spoon, a lid, and a burger smasher or spatula. Place all of your ingredients on a tray so they're ready to go.

LET'S DO IT!

1 Set up the grill for direct cooking. Preheat to 400°F (204°C). Place a large cast-iron skillet on the grates.

2 Place two ground beef balls on the hot skillet. Use the burger smasher to smash the balls flat. Cook just until the juices begin to flow.

3 Move the burgers to one side of the skillet and place the bun halves, split sides down, in the skillet and directly into the rendered fat. (If the skillet isn't large enough to hold the buns, you can toast them directly on the grill grates. Just watch them carefully, as they will toast very quickly.)

4 Remove the toasted bun halves from the skillet. Liberally season the burgers with kosher salt and black pepper and then flip them.

5 Add 3 tablespoons butter, 1 thyme sprig, and 1 garlic clove to the skillet. Use a spoon to baste the burgers continuously in the butter for 1 minute.

6 Place a cheese slice on top of each burger, and then cover with the lid to help the cheese melt more quickly.

7 While the cheese is melting, drizzle the burger sauce over the split sides of the buns. Place the patties on the bottom bun, and then top with the crown.

8 Carefully wipe the skillet clean with paper towels to remove any burned bits, and then repeat the process with the remaining ingredients to make the second burger. Serve immediately!

DO IT LIKE GUGA!

The cooking process happens very quickly, so make sure you prep everything ahead of time and have it right next to you as you prepare to cook. You can easily scale this recipe up to make as many burgers as you like; I usually like to make 5 or 6 at a time. If you do cook multiple burgers, be sure to wipe the cast-iron skillet clean between cooking each burger so you don't end up with any burned bits on the next burgers you cook.

GARLIC BREAD FILET MIGNON
STEAK SANDWICH

The combination of garlic and steak is always a perfect match. And when you combine those flavors into an amazing sandwich, it creates an absolute perfection of those flavors!

3 (10oz/283g) filet mignons

Coarse kosher salt

Ground black pepper

Garlic powder

3 sandwich-sized Italian bread loaves, sliced lengthwise

8 tbsp butter, melted

Pickled Red Onions (p. 187)

FOR THE GARLIC BUTTER

8 tbsp room-temperature butter

1 tbsp garlic paste

1 tbsp chopped fresh parsley

FOR THE SRIRACHA MAYO

3 tbsp mayonnaise

½ tbsp sriracha sauce

1 tsp lemon juice

1 tsp minced garlic

PREP AND SEASONING

1   Liberally season all sides of the filets with kosher salt, black pepper, and garlic powder. (Be sure to season both sides as well as the edges.) Set aside.

2   Make the garlic butter by combining the butter, garlic paste, and parsley in a small bowl. Mix well to combine. Set aside.

3   Make the sriracha mayo by combining the mayonnaise, sriracha sauce, lemon juice, and garlic in a small bowl. Mix well to combine. Set aside.

TIP   *Try to have everything prepped ahead so that cooking the steaks is the final step. This will ensure the steaks don't sit while the other components are being prepared.*

LET'S DO IT!

1   Set up the grill for two-zone cooking. Preheat to 250°F (121°C).

2   Place the steaks over indirect heat. Cook, turning them occasionally, until they reach an internal temperature of 125°F (52°C), about 30 minutes to 1 hour.

3   While the steaks are cooking, preheat the oven broiler. Spread the garlic butter over the cut sides of the bread, making sure to cover all of the edges. Place the bread pieces cut sides up on a baking tray and place them in the oven. Toast until golden brown.

4   Once the steaks reach temperature, move them to direct heat to give them a nice sear and a nice crust. Once you have a nice crust, baste them with the melted butter to finish them off.

5   Remove the steaks from the grill and set aside to rest for 5 to 10 minutes before slicing thinly.

6   Place the steak slices on the bottom halves of the loaves. Top with a spoonful of the pickled onions. Spread a spoonful of the sriracha mayo over the cut sides of the crowns, and then place the crowns on the sandwiches.

DO IT LIKE GUGA!

If you like to experiment, try cooking each filet mignon using a different method. You can grill one, smoke one, and then cook one sous vide. This will give everyone a unique taste experience and a special way to try different flavors!

BONE MARROW CHEESE-STEAK

After a cheeseburger, the cheesesteak is one of my absolute favorite sandwiches. The original cheesesteak is an all-time classic and was created in Philadelphia in the 1930s. This recipe is my unique spin on this classic, with the addition of something that takes it to the next level—Butter of the Gods!

14oz (397g) whole ribeye

1 tbsp beef tallow

1 medium white onion, chopped

Coarse kosher salt

Ground black pepper

1 (15oz/425g) jar Cheez Whiz

2 French baguettes, split (you can also use whatever crusty bread you prefer)

4 tbsp Butter of the Gods (p. 202)

4 slices provolone cheese

PREP AND SEASONING

1   Using a sharp knife, remove all of the silver skin and connective tissue from the ribeye. Transfer to the freezer for 45 minutes to allow it to firm up.

2   After 45 minutes, remove the ribeye from the freezer and slice it into thin pieces. Chop the pieces into smaller chunks. (Don't chop it too much, you don't want to end up with ground beef!)

TIP *If you want to make this recipe less expensively, you can use brisket or top sirloin in place of the whole ribeye, but it won't be as good unless you supplement the meat with some additional beef fat.*

LET'S DO IT!

1   Set up the grill for direct cooking. Preheat to 350°F (177°C). Place a large cast-iron skillet on the grill grate.

2   Add the beef tallow to the hot skillet. Once the tallow is melted, add the onions. Sauté just until the onions are lightly browned and then remove from the skillet. Set aside.

3   Immediately add the meat to the skillet. Season liberally with kosher salt and black pepper. Cook until the meat is browned and cooked through, about 3 to 4 minutes.

4   While the meat is cooking, add the Cheez Whiz to a medium saucepan over medium-low heat. Heat the Cheez Whiz until it's smooth and pourable. Set aside.

5   Once the meat is fully cooked, add the onions back to the skillet. Continue cooking until the onions are soft.

6   Once the onions are cooked, push all of the meat and onions to the middle of the skillet and place the bottoms of the hoagie rolls on top of the meat so they can heat up for a minute or two. Use a spatula to invert the meat and rolls to a plate.

7   Place 2 tablespoons of the Butter of the Gods on top of the meat on each sandwich. Top each sandwich with 2 slices of provolone cheese and then drizzle the warm Cheez Whiz over the provolone cheese. Place the tops of the rolls on the sandwiches. Serve hot.

CUBANO SANDWICH

The Cuban sandwich is a staple around Miami; you can find it at nearly any restaurant. It has a unique combination of fillings that just seem like they belong together, and they're always topped with the amazing Cuban bread. This is a must-try if you're ever in Miami, but I'm going to show you how to make these sandwiches yourself!

7–10lb (3.18–4.54kg) picnic pork shoulder

Yellow mustard

20 slices Cuban bread (about 2 loaves)

20 slices Swiss cheese

1lb (454g) old-fashioned deli ham, thinly sliced

About 30 dill or sweet pickle slices, chopped

¼ cup butter

FOR THE MARINADE

Juice of 4 sour oranges (or juice of 3 navel oranges and 1 lime)

½ cup water

½ cup white wine

10 garlic cloves

Juice of 4 limes

4 tbsp soy sauce

4 tbsp smoked paprika

4 tbsp apple cider vinegar

4 tbsp olive oil

3 tbsp coarse kosher salt

PREP AND SEASONING

1   Using a paring knife, poke holes over the entire meat side of the pork shoulder. (Make sure you do not go too deep and puncture the skin.)

2   Make the marinade by combining the ingredients in a blender. Blend until well combined.

3   Place the pork shoulder in a large vacuum bag or large freezer bag. Add the marinade, seal the bag, carefully turn the bag to coat the shoulder in the marinade. Place the pork shoulder in the fridge to marinate for 24 hours.

4   Once the marinating time is complete, remove the pork shoulder from the fridge and discard the bag, but reserve the marinade. Place the pork shoulder on a large-rimmed baking tray lined with aluminum foil.

5   Use paper towels to pat the skin dry and then use a paring knife to poke small holes in the skin to allow the moisture to release. Pour some of the reserved marinade into the bottom of the tray.

6   Place the pork shoulder back in the fridge. Refrigerate, uncovered, for an additional 12 hours to dry out the skin.

TIP *Cuban bread can be found in most Latin grocery stores. If you can't find it, you can substitute soft breads like hoagie rolls or French baguettes.*

LET'S DO IT!

1   Set up the grill for indirect heat. Preheat to 375°F (191°C).

2   Place the pork shoulder on the grill. Cook until it reaches an internal temperature of 205°F (96°C), about 4 to 8 hours.

3   Once the pork shoulder reaches temperature, remove it from the grill and then use a flamethrower or oven broiler to crisp the skin.

4   Set the pork shoulder aside to rest for at least 30 minutes. After 30 minutes, shred or chop the meat into small pieces. Reserve the juices from the cutting board and add them back to the meat.

5   To assemble the sandwiches, spread a layer of yellow mustard over a slice of bread and then top with a layer of the pork, 2 slices Swiss cheese, a layer of the ham, and a layer of the pickles. Butter the outside of the second slice of bread and place on top of the sandwich.

6   Place a sandwich in a sandwich press and cook until the bread is toasted and the cheese has melted. (Alternatively, you can place the sandwich in a hot skillet and place a second skillet on top of the sandwich to press it.) Repeat with the remaining sandwiches.

DO IT LIKE GUGA!

If you have the time, let the meat rest in the oven overnight on the lowest setting, ideally around 150°F (66°C). This will keep the juices from escaping and will result in even better flavor!

COW TONGUE TACOS

Don't knock this recipe until you try it! This recipe may sound a bit weird, but don't let it scare you; this is a very popular dish in many countries around the world, and it's for good reason: it's delicious! You might be surprised to find that this becomes your new favorite style of tacos!

5–8lb (2.27–3.63kg) cow tongue

6 ½ cups (1.5L) beef tallow

1 head of garlic

1 cinnamon stick

3 chile morita (smoked and dried red jalapeños)

1 tbsp avocado oil (or Wagyu fat)

Coarse kosher salt and ground black pepper, to taste

FOR SERVING

15–30 small corn tortillas

Birria Tacos Green Sauce (p. 207)

Mexican crema

1 cup chopped fresh cilantro

1 cup chopped white onion

PREP AND SEASONING

1 Trim any excess fat from the bottom of the cow tongue.

2 Preheat the oven to 250°F (121°C).

3 Add the beef tallow to a large pot. Place it in the hot oven until fully melted.

4 When the tallow is melted, remove the pot from the oven and add the tongue, garlic head, cinnamon stick, and chile morita to the pot.

LET'S DO IT!

1 Preheat the smoker to 250°F (121°C).

2 Place the pot with the tongue in the smoker. Smoke for 3 to 4 hours or until the skin easily peels away from the rest of the meat.

3 Remove the skin from the tongue, and then set it aside to rest for at least 10 minutes. Discard the skin and dice the meat into small pieces.

4 Place a large skillet over high heat. Add the avocado oil and then add the diced tongue. Toss until the tongue develops a nice crust. Season with kosher salt and black pepper to taste.

5 To assemble the tacos, add a scoop of the tongue to a tortilla. (How much you want to add is up to you. You can add more or less, depending on how many you are serving.) Drizzle the Birria Tacos Green Sauce and Mexican crema over the tongue, and then top with a pinch of cilantro and a spoonful of onion.

DO IT LIKE GUGA!

If you have a tortilla press at home and want to make your own tortillas, combine 1 part butter, 10 parts maseca corn flour, and 2 parts water in a large bowl. (It's impossible to give exact amounts, so just go by look and feel as I do!) Mix until the dough forms a dough-like consistency. (If it's too dry, add more water in small amounts.) Shape the dough into small balls. Place the balls on a tortilla press and press them flat. Cook the tortillas in a hot cast-iron skillet until they develop a nice golden-brown color on each side.

GUGA'S BURGER BUNS

I share with you the best hamburger bun recipe ever. These take a little work to make, but they are absolutely worth it. I've made them countless times and have tweaked the recipe over the years to ensure perfect results. These buns are always a big hit with everyone and will work with any kind of sandwich, not just burgers!

463g all-purpose flour

14g baker's yeast

31g granulated sugar

30g Nido (or other whole milk powder)

9g fine table salt

41g melted butter

220g lukewarm water

2 large eggs, divided

1–2 tbsp olive oil

Sesame seeds (for topping)

LET'S DO IT!

1   Combine the flour, yeast, sugar, Nido, and table salt in a large bowl. Mix well to combine.

2   Add the melted butter, lukewarm water, and 1 egg. Continue mixing until the ingredients are well combined and form a dough. Shape the dough into a ball.

3   Lightly coat the interior of another large bowl with olive oil. Place the dough ball in the bowl, cover with plastic wrap, and set aside in a warm location to rise for about 2 hours or until the dough doubles in size.

4   Place the dough on a lightly floured surface. Use a rolling pin to roll it flat, and then cut it into 6 equal-sized pieces. Roll each piece into a ball.

5   Line a large baking tray with parchment paper. Place the balls on the tray and then brush them with the olive oil. Again cover them in plastic wrap, and set them aside to rise for 1 more hour.

6   Preheat the oven to 425°F (218°C).

7   Add the remaining egg to a small bowl, and then whisk to combine. Brush the buns with the egg wash, and then sprinkle some sesame seeds over the top of the buns.

8   Place the buns in the oven. Bake for about 20 minutes or until the tops are golden brown.

9   When you're ready to serve, slice the buns in half, spread a little butter over the cut sides, and toast them up on the grill.

TIP *For even better flavor, let the dough rest in the refrigerator overnight for the first rise.*

DO IT LIKE GUGA!

If you have burger bun rings, use them when letting the dough rise the second time and also when you bake the buns. They will help the buns gain more height and also create more uniform shapes.

SHORT RIB TACOS

If you've only eaten carryout tacos, you absolutely have to try this recipe. You'll never buy carryout tacos again! Making these tacos does take some time, but it is so worth the effort.

4–6lb (1.80–2.75kg) 4-bone short rib

2 cups beef stock

12 small corn tortillas

1 cup chopped fresh cilantro

1 cup chopped white onion

Spicy Red Taco Sauce (p. 209)

FOR THE MARINADE

5 guajillo chiles

Juice of 4 sour oranges (or juice of 3 navel oranges and 1 lime)

¼ cup white vinegar

1 cup pineapple juice

5 garlic cloves

2 medium white onions

1 tbsp ground cinnamon

1 tbsp white pepper

1 tbsp ground black pepper

1 tbsp dried oregano

1 tbsp cumin

4 tbsp achiote powder

FOR THE AVOCADO SAUCE

1 medium avocado

Juice of half a lime

1 tbsp chopped fresh cilantro

1 tsp ground black pepper

2 tbsp mayonnaise

2 tbsp Mexican crema

1 tsp coarse kosher salt

PREP AND SEASONING

1   Begin making the marinade by filling a medium pan with water. Bring the water to a boil over high heat.

2   Add the guajillo chiles to the boiling water. Boil for 30 seconds to 1 minute to rehydrate the chiles.

3   Add the chiles to a blender along with the remaining marinade ingredients. Blend until the ingredients are well combined.

LET'S DO IT!

1   Preheat the smoker to 250°F (121°C).

2   Use a flamethrower to sear the ribs on both sides until golden brown. (You're just looking to give them a nice golden-brown color at this stage, not to fully cook them. You can also sear the ribs in a hot cast-iron skillet placed over high heat.)

3   Place the short ribs in a medium pot. Add the beef stock, and then pour the marinade over the ribs.

4   Place the pot with the ribs in the smoker. Cook until the ribs reach an internal temperature of 205°F (96°C), about 6 to 8 hours.

5   When the ribs are close to being done cooking, make the avocado sauce by combining all of the ingredients in a blender. Blend until the ingredients are well combined and smooth. Set aside.

6   When the ribs are done cooking, remove them from the smoker and reserve the cooking liquid. Remove the ribs from the pot, shred the meat, and then combine the meat with some of the cooking liquid.

7   To assemble the tacos, add a generous portion of the meat to a tortilla, followed by a pinch of the cilantro, a spoonful of the onion, and a drizzle of the avocado sauce. Top with the Spicy Red Taco Sauce.

DO IT LIKE GUGA!

For an even more flavorful bite, skip searing the ribs and let the meat marinate overnight in the fridge. You will lose the flavor from the sear, but the meat will gain a more intense flavor from the marinade that is absolutely irreplaceable!

HOMEMADE BACON
BLT SANDWICH

There are few things in life that are better than bacon! And making your own homemade bacon is even better. You will be able to flavor the bacon however you please, it will taste a thousand times better than any store-bought bacon, and it will make absolutely incredible BLT sandwiches!

5–7lb (2.27–3.18kg) skinless pork belly

10–12 slices soft white bread

½ cup mayonnaise

1 medium head iceberg lettuce

2 large tomatoes, sliced

Pinch of coarse kosher salt

Pinch of ground black pepper

FOR THE BRINE

½ cup brown sugar

½ cup sea salt

½ cup maple syrup

½ cup ponzu sauce

¼ tsp pink curing salt

PREP AND SEASONING

1   Make the brine by combining the brown sugar, sea salt, maple syrup, ponzu sauce, and pink curing salt in a large bowl. (For saltier bacon, omit the maple syrup.) Stir well to combine.

2   Add the pork belly to a vacuum bag or large freezer bag. Pour in the brine and seal the bag or remove as much air as possible. Transfer the pork belly to the fridge to brine for 5 to 7 days.

3   After the brining time is complete, remove the pork belly from the bag. Discard the bag along with the liquids.

4   Rinse the pork belly three times with cold water to remove as much of the brine as possible. (If you don't rinse off the brine, the pork belly will be super salty.)

5   Place the pork belly on a wire cooling rack and then place the rack on a baking tray. (If you don't do this, the grease from the pork belly can start a fire in your smoker.)

TIP   *Adding the pink curing salt to the brine will help the bacon last longer. If you're going to eat the bacon right away, omit the pink salt in the brine. The pink curing salt is not used for seasoning, it is only used to help preserve the meat for a longer period of time.*

LET'S DO IT!

1   Preheat the smoker to 250°F (121°C).

2   Place the pork belly in the smoker. Smoke until it reaches an internal temperature of 155°F (68°C), about 1 to 4 hours.

3   Once the pork belly reaches the desired temperature, remove it from the smoker. Set it aside to rest for 30 minutes to 1 hour.

4   While the bacon is resting, toast the bread slices. Set aside.

5   Set up the grill for direct heat. Preheat to 400°F (204°C).

6   Slice the pork belly into strips. (Only slice as much as you will need for the sandwiches, about 12–15 strips). Place the strips on the hot grill and cook until they're nice and crispy, about 5 to 10 minutes.

7   To assemble the sandwiches, spread a spoonful of mayonnaise over a toasted slice of bread. Add a few crisp lettuce leaves, followed by the bacon slices and then a few tomato slices. Lightly sprinkle kosher salt and black pepper over the tomato slices and then top the sandwich with another slice of toasted bread. Repeat with the remaining ingredients.

8   Refrigerate the uncut bacon in a resealable bag for up to 10 days.

SMOKED CRISPY
CHICKEN SANDWICH

Something special happens when you deep-fry and then smoke chicken—the flavor that the smoke produces is unmatched! This isn't just a regular chicken sandwich—you are going to love it!

---

5 boneless, skinless chicken thighs

1 tsp coarse kosher salt

16fl oz (473mL) buttermilk

4 cups canola or peanut oil (for frying)

5 hamburger buns

FOR THE SEASONING BLEND

⅔ tsp coarse kosher salt

½ tsp dried thyme

½ tsp dried basil

⅓ tsp dried oregano

1 tsp celery salt

1 tsp ground black pepper

1 tsp dry mustard

4 tsp smoked paprika

2 tsp granulated garlic

1 tsp ground ginger

3 tsp white pepper

¾ tsp Homemade MSG Seasoning (p. 217) or store-bought MSG seasoning

FOR THE DREDGING MIX

5 tbsp corn starch

5 tbsp all-purpose flour

4 tsp smoked paprika

2 tsp granulated garlic

½ tsp ground black pepper

1 tsp coarse kosher salt

PREP AND SEASONING

1   Making the seasoning blend by combining the ingredients in a medium bowl. Mix well.

2   Season the chicken thighs with the kosher salt, and then coat liberally with the seasoning blend. Transfer the seasoned chicken thighs to a large bowl, and then pour in the buttermilk. Cover the bowl and place the chicken in the fridge to marinate for at least 8 hours or overnight.

3   Make the dredging mix by combining the ingredients in a shallow tray. Set aside.

TIP *If you want to get a bit crazy, try deep-frying the chicken in Wagyu beef tallow or even duck fat! This will add incredible flavor to your sandwich and really take it over the top.*

LET'S DO IT!

1   Preheat the smoker to 400°F (204°C).

2   Remove the chicken from the bowl. Shake gently to remove any excess buttermilk.

3   Dredge the chicken thighs in the seasoned flour until thoroughly coated. Shake lightly to remove any excess mix, and then transfer to a cooling rack.

4   Place a medium cast-iron pan over medium-high heat. Add the cooking oil and heat it to 350°F (177°C). Carefully place the thighs in the hot oil. Fry until the thighs develop a nice golden-brown color, about 2 minutes, and then transfer the thighs to a plate.

5   Place the thighs in the smoker. Smoke for 1 hour or until the chicken reaches an internal temperature of 175°F (79°C).

6   Split the hamburger buns. Set aside.

7   When the thighs have reached temperature, remove them from the smoker and place them on the buns. Add whatever toppings you like. (I like to add spicy mayo, along with cole slaw, pickles, or pickled red onions.)

HEART ATTACK BURGER

This burger will not make your doctor happy, but it will definitely make your belly happy! Breakfast, lunch and dinner—this burger has it all and then some! It's an absolute showstopper! (And a heart-stopper!)

1½lb (680g) chopped brisket

1½lb (680g) chopped chuck roast

1lb (454g) trimmed uncooked beef fat (preferably trimmed Wagyu fat)

Coarse kosher salt

Ground black pepper

Garlic powder

5 medium chorizo sausage links (preferably Argentinian), partially split lengthwise

15 slices uncooked bacon

5 medium eggs

10 slices American cheese

10 slices pepper jack cheese

5 Guga's Burger Buns (p. 145) or store-bought burger buns

FOR THE GUACAMOLE

2 large avocados, diced

2 large red tomatoes, seeded and diced

1 small red onion, diced

1 red jalapeño, seeded and diced

2 tbsp chopped fresh cilantro

2 tbsp Red Chimichurri Sauce (p. 211)

Juice of 2 medium limes

Coarse kosher salt and ground black pepper, to taste

PREP AND SEASONING

1 Combine the brisket, chuck roast, and beef fat in a food processor. Process until well combined. Shape the mixture into 10 (6oz/170g) patties. Set aside.

2 Make the guacamole by combining the avocados, tomatoes, onion, red jalapeño, cilantro, Red Chimichurri Sauce, and lime juice in a large bowl. Mix well and then season with kosher salt and black pepper to taste. Cover and transfer to the fridge. (And try not to eat it all before the cook is complete because it is delicious!)

LET'S DO IT!

1 Set up the grill for direct cooking. Preheat to 375°F (191°C).

2 Place a large cast-iron skillet on the grill grate. When the skillet is hot, place the burgers in the skillet and season liberally with kosher salt, black pepper, and garlic powder.

3 While the burgers are cooking, place the chorizo links split sides down on the grill grate. Cook the sausages until they reach an internal temperature of 165°F (74°C), about 15 to 20 minutes.

4 While the burgers and sausages are cooking, place a second cast-iron skillet on the grates. Add the bacon and cook just until the fat is bubbling and the bacon is crispy on the edges. Transfer the cooked bacon and grilled sausages to a paper towel–lined plate to drain.

5 Add the eggs to the same skillet that was used to cook the bacon. (If there isn't enough rendered fat, add a small amount of vegetable oil to the skillet.) Fry the eggs until they're cooked "over easy" and still have runny yolks. Place the eggs on the plate with the bacon and sausages.

6 When the burgers are almost ready, top each patty with a slice of American cheese, followed by a slice of pepper jack cheese. Allow the cheese to melt before removing the patties from the heat.

7 Assemble the burgers by spreading a nice layer of the guacamole on the bottom bun, followed a burger patty, and then a slice of the chorizo. Top with another patty, followed by a fried egg, three slices of bacon, and then the top bun. Serve hot.

DO IT LIKE GUGA!

The hamburger blend in this recipe absolutely takes the flavor to the next level. However, if you prefer to use regular ground beef, I recommend buying a high-quality organic ground beef that has a meat-to-fat ratio of 80/20.

SMOKED
PORK BELLY SANDWICH

This amazing smoked pork belly sandwich is not only the best I've ever tasted, it's truly something I wish I could eat every single day. What makes it so good is that the flavors are so perfectly balanced.

5lb (2.25kg) pork belly

Coarse kosher salt

Guga's BBQ Rub (p. 200)

6 medium eggs

6 Guga's Burger Buns (p. 145) or store-bought burger buns

Pickled Korean Cucumbers (p. 184)

Small bunch of fresh cilantro, stems removed

FOR THE CHEESE SPREAD

½ cup shredded mozzarella cheese

2 tbsp cream cheese

2 tbsp Mexican crema

2 tbsp chopped fresh chives

FOR THE CARAMELIZED ONIONS

2 tbsp olive oil

1 large white onion, thinly sliced

1 tbsp oyster sauce

2 tbsp soy sauce

PREP AND SEASONING

1   Place the pork belly on a cooling rack that is placed on a large baking tray. Season all sides liberally with coarse kosher salt and Guga's BBQ Rub. Transfer to the fridge to rest while you prepare the cheese spread and get the smoker ready.

2   Combine the mozzarella cheese, cream cheese, Mexican crema, and chives in a food processor. Process until a paste is formed. Set aside.

TIP *For an even more tender result and even better seasoning, try dry brining the pork belly overnight prior to grilling or smoking.*

LET'S DO IT!

1   Preheat the smoker to 250°F (121°C).

2   Place the pork belly in the smoker. Smoke for 4 hours or until the internal temperature reaches 165°F (74°C).

3   While the pork belly is smoking, make the caramelized onions by placing a large skillet over medium-low heat. Add the olive oil. When the oil is hot, add the onions. Cook until the onions develop a nice golden-brown color, and then deglaze the pan with 1 to 2 tablespoons of water. Cook the onions for another 2 minutes, and then add the oyster sauce and soy sauce. Stir to combine and then transfer the caramelized onions to a bowl. Set aside.

4   In the same pan used to fry the onions, fry the eggs and then set aside. (I like to fry the eggs sunny-side up, but you can cook them however you prefer.)

5   When the pork belly is done smoking, take it out of the smoker and place it in a warm oven set to its lowest setting, to rest for about 30 minutes. After 30 minutes, slice the pork belly into 1-inch-thick (2.5cm thick) strips.

6   Place a large cast-iron skillet over medium-high heat. Add the sliced pork belly to the hot skllet. Sear the pieces just long enough to add a nice crust.

7   Split the buns. Spread a generous portion of the cheese spread over the bottom bun. Add some caramelized onions, followed by 4 pieces of pork belly, a fried egg, a spoonful of pickled cucumbers, and a sprinkling of the cilantro leaves. Add another layer of the cheese spread to the top bun and then top the sandwich with the top bun.

DO IT LIKE GUGA!

I like to smoke the pork belly ahead of time but skip the searing step and just store it in the fridge. When I'm ready to serve, I just sear the pieces I want and leave the remaining pieces in the fridge. This ensures the pieces are always hot and have a nice crust!

EXTRAS

ROASTED BONE MARROW

If you haven't tried roasted bone marrow, you simply haven't been to Food Heaven. There is a good reason why I like to call this "meat butter"—the flavor is unmatched and it literally makes everything taste better, whether it's eaten on its own or added to another dish. This one may seem a little scary to some, but I highly recommend you give it a try! You will become a believer!

½ gallon (1.90L) water

½ cup table salt

2 beef bone marrow canoes

Coarse kosher salt

Ground black pepper

1 tsp garlic powder

1 tsp chili powder

1 tsp finely diced shallots

1 tsp shredded Parmesan cheese

1 tsp finely diced fresh chives

PREP AND SEASONING

1   Combine the water and table salt in a medium bowl. Stir until the salt is fully dissolved.

2   Place the bone marrow canoes in the water. Transfer to the fridge for at least 24 hours and up to 3 days. (This process removes the blood from the marrow. The longer you leave the bones in the water, the more blood will be extracted.)

3   Once the blood is extracted from the bone marrow, remove the canoes from the water and pat them dry with paper towels.

4   Season liberally with the kosher salt and black pepper, and then season lightly with the garlic powder and chili powder. Place the canoes on a large baking tray and sprinkle the shallots over the top.

LET'S DO IT!

1   Preheat the broiler to high.

2   Place the bone marrow canoes on the middle rack of the oven. Roast for 10 minutes.

3   Remove from the oven. Sprinkle the Parmesan and chives over the top. Serve warm.

DO IT LIKE GUGA!

Pair this with some garlic bread, Simple Vinaigrette Salad (p. 197), and a beautiful steak. Try to choose a steak that isn't too fatty, like a filet mignon, so that it will balance out the richness of the bone marrow. This is one recipe that will have everyone asking for more!

RACK OF LAMB

There is a huge difference between imported lamb and domestic lamb. When I first started my YouTube channel, my nephew, Angel, would never eat lamb. That was until I discovered domestic lamb from my meat dealer, Emilio. Imported lamb can be gamy, but domestic lamb has a milder flavor. Nowadays, Angel always asks me to make lamb!

2lb (907g) whole rack domestic lamb

8 tbsp salted butter

FOR THE MARINADE

1 tsp fresh thyme

2 garlic cloves

1 tsp sriracha sauce

1 tsp dried parsley

1 tbsp Worcestershire sauce

1 tbsp sherry vinegar

2 tsp coarse kosher salt

1 tbsp lemon zest

1 tsp lemon juice

1 tsp black pepper

1 tbsp olive oil

PREP AND SEASONING

1   Pat the rack dry with paper towels. Stand the rack bones-side up, and then slice into 8 individual chops. Set aside.

2   Combine the marinade ingredients in a food processor. Process on high until well combined and no chunks remain.

3   Add the chops to a vacuum bag or resealable plastic bag. Add the marinade, seal the bag, and then gently turn the bag to coat the chops in the marinade. Transfer to the fridge to marinate overnight.

TIP *If you use a vacuum chamber bag or a FoodSaver bag to marinate the meat, it can cut the marinating time by two-thirds because the vacuum seal will force the marinade deeper into the meat.*

LET'S DO IT!

1   Remove the chops from the marinade. Discard the bag and marinade.

2   Set up the grill for direct cooking. Preheat the grill to 450°F (232°C). (Get this thing hot! If you're using charcoal, you'll want the coals to be about 3 inches (7.5cm) from the grill grates. If you're using gas, preheat the grill to high.)

3   While the grill is preheating, add the butter to a small saucepan over medium-low heat. Heat the butter until melted. Set aside.

4   Place the chops on the hot grill grates. Sear for 2 to 3 minutes per side, turning them frequently, until the chops are golden brown and the internal temperature reaches 135°F (57°C). (These will cook quickly, so keep a close eye on them.)

5   Remove the chops from the grill and set aside to rest for 5 to 10 minutes so they can reach the final temperature of 140°F (60°C).

6   While the chops are resting, baste them with the melted butter. Serve warm. (If desired, serve with Roasted Garlic Mashed Potatoes [p. 176] on the side.) Serve warm.

DO IT LIKE GUGA!

If you want to take the flavor up another notch, add 1 teaspoon Homemade MSG Seasoning (p. 217) to the marinade.

HEAVEN'S FISH
(3 WAYS)

This recipe was inspired by my favorite restaurant in the Florida Keys, Lazy Days. With this recipe, you get to try this delicious fish three different ways: savory (with the lazy topping), sweet (with the tropical topping), and spicy (with the jalapeño topping). If you don't want to make all three toppings, you can just triple the recipe for whichever topping you prefer, but you'll be missing out!

2lb (907g) hogfish, cut into six filets
Guga's BBQ Rub (p. 200)
8 tbsp butter
1 tbsp garlic paste

FOR THE LAZY TOPPING

1 cup diced tomatoes
¼ cup finely chopped green onion
1 tbsp finely chopped red onion

FOR THE TROPICAL TOPPING

½ cup finely chopped mango
½ cup finely chopped pineapple
1 tbsp finely chopped fresh chives

FOR THE JALAPEÑO TOPPING

1 tbsp finely diced jalapeños
8 tbsp butter
1 tbsp garlic paste
1 cup unseasoned bread crumbs

PREP AND SEASONING

1   Liberally season both sides of the filets with Guga's BBQ Rub.

2   Make the lazy topping by combining the ingredients in a small bowl. Cover with plastic wrap and transfer to the fridge.

3   Make the tropical topping by combining the ingredients in a small bowl. Cover with plastic wrap and transfer to the fridge.

4   Combine the butter and garlic paste in a small pan over medium heat. Stir and heat until the butter is melted and the garlic is fragrant. Set aside.

LET'S DO IT!

1   Preheat the smoker to 250°F (121°C).

2   Place the fish filets in the smoker. Smoke until the fish reaches an internal temperature of 145°F (63°C), about 20 to 30 minutes.

3   While the fish is smoking, make the jalapeño topping by placing a medium skillet over medium heat. Add the jalapeños, butter, garlic paste, and bread crumbs. Sauté until the jalapeños are soft and the bread crumbs are golden brown.

4   When the fish is done smoking, remove it from the smoker and divide the filets into three separate serving dishes. Top one serving with the jalapeño topping, top the second serving with the tropical topping, and top the third serving with the lazy topping.

5   Drizzle the melted garlic butter over the top of each dish. Serve hot.

DO IT LIKE GUGA!

If you don't want to smoke the fish, you can simply coat it with bread crumbs and panfry it. It will still taste amazing!

SMOKED BBQ "CANNOLI"

If you want to make a side dish that nobody will expect but everyone will absolutely love, this is the one. It's made with manicotti, so it's not really cannoli, but I consider this my unique BBQ twist on that Italian classic treat! It takes a little time to make, but it's definitely worth the effort.

8 manicotti pasta tubes

2 cups shredded Cheddar cheese

2 cups shredded mozzarella

½ lb (227g) ground beef

1 tbsp chopped fresh parsley

3 garlic cloves, minced

2 tbsp chopped shallots

1 medium seedless jalapeño, diced

1 (8oz/227g) package cream cheese

Coarse kosher salt, to taste

Ground black pepper, to taste

8 slices uncooked bacon
  (about ½ lb/227g)

2 cups Guga's BBQ Sauce (p. 201),
  divided

2 tsp chopped fresh parsley

PREP AND SEASONING

1   Cook the pasta according to package directions. Drain and set aside.

2   Combine the Cheddar, mozzarella, ground beef, parsley, garlic, shallots, and jalapeño in a food processor. Process until the ingredients are well combined and a paste is formed.

3   Add the cream cheese and process again until well combined. Season to taste with kosher salt and black pepper.

4   Gently stuff the manicotti tubes with the filling and then wrap each tube with a slice of bacon. Place the stuffed tubes on a wire cooling rack. Transfer to the fridge while you get the smoker ready.

TIP *You can prepare everything up to a day in advance of smoking, but be sure to tightly cover the manicotti in plastic wrap so they don't dry out.*

LET'S DO IT!

1   Remove the stuffed tubes from the fridge. Preheat the smoker to 300°F (149°C).

2   Place the stuffed tubes and cooling rack in the smoker. Smoke for 40 to 45 minutes or until the bacon is golden brown.

3   Continue smoking for an additional 15 minutes, brushing the tubes with the sauce every 5 minutes.

4   While the "cannoli" are finishing in the smoker, add the remaining ½ cup of Guga's BBQ Sauce to a small saucepan over medium-low heat. Heat until hot.

5   Remove the "cannoli" from the smoker. Place in a serving dish, and drizzle the remaining sauce over the top. Sprinkle the chopped parsley over the top. Serve warm. (This is delicious served with garlic bread on the side.)

TIP *If you don't have a smoker, you can still make this in your oven. Just bake in a preheated oven at 300°F (149°C) for 40 to 45 minutes.*

CAVIAR COMPOUND BUTTER

Caviar is one of the world's best-known delicacies. The flavor is absolutely phenomenal, and when you combine it with butter, it turns this amazing delicacy into something that will take any dish you make over the top. This simple preparation will make you look like a really fancy chef!

2oz (57g) Kaluga caviar (or any other variety of caviar you prefer)

8 tbsp salted butter (room temperature)

LET'S DO IT!

1   Combine the caviar and butter in a small bowl.

2   Using a spoon, very gently combine the ingredients.

3   Place the caviar butter on a piece of plastic wrap. Roll it up tightly and shape it into a log.

4   Transfer to the fridge to solidify for 1 to 2 hours.

5   After 1 to 2 hours, slice and serve the butter however you like. Store in the fridge for up to 1 week.

LEFTOVER BRISKET

HUEVOS RANCHEROS

The saying that some foods taste better the next day is absolutely true for this dish. It's an easy yet delicious breakfast meal that will use up any leftover brisket you have on hand. And the brisket is really just the cherry on top.

12 small cherry tomatoes

4 garlic cloves

1 tsp coarse kosher salt

1 (16oz/454g) can refried beans

1lb (454g) chopped smoked brisket

1 medium white onion, diced

4 tbsp finely chopped fresh cilantro, divided

Coarse kosher salt and ground black pepper, to taste

4 large flour tortillas

4 medium eggs

4 tbsp crumbled cotija cheese

PREP AND SEASONING

1 Char the tomatoes over an open flame to give them some color. (Since these are small tomatoes, a Searzall or culinary torch will make the job easier. You can also char them in a small skillet on the stove top.)

2 Add the garlic cloves and kosher salt to a food processor. Process until the garlic is finely chopped, and then add the charred tomatoes. Process until the tomatoes are thoroughly mashed and well combined with the garlic.

3 Place the refried beans in a medium saucepan over medium heat. Heat until warm. Stir and set aside.

LET'S DO IT!

1 Place a large cast-iron skillet over medium heat. Add the brisket to the skillet along with the onion and 2 tablespoons cilantro.

2 Once the brisket is heated through, add the tomato-garlic mixture and then stir well to combine. Season with kosher salt and black pepper to taste. Remove the brisket from the skillet.

3 Crack the eggs into the skillet, and fry until they are scrambled (or cooked to your liking).

4 Once the eggs are cooked, briefly place the tortillas in the hot skillet to warm them. Transfer the warm tortillas to plates.

5 To serve, spread the refried beans over a tortilla, place some of the eggs on top of the beans, followed by a generous portion of the brisket. Sprinkle 1 tablespoon cotija cheese over the brisket, followed by a sprinkle of the cilantro. Roll the tortilla into a burrito. Repeat with the remaining tortillas.

CHEESY BACON GNOCCHI

Gnocchi is one of my favorite pastas, and this recipe takes it to another level. It's a quick and easy dish that will please everyone and have them begging for more. Come on! There's bacon, cheese, pasta, and mushrooms! What's not to love?!

2 packages (16oz/454g each) potato gnocchi

½ cup chopped uncooked bacon (about 2–3 strips)

3 cups sliced baby portobello mushrooms

1½ cups heavy cream

1 tbsp garlic paste

½ cup shredded Parmesan cheese

2 cups shredded smoked Gouda cheese

LET'S DO IT!

1   Cook the gnocchi according to package directions. Drain and set aside.

2   Add the bacon to a large skillet over medium heat. Fry until nice and crispy. Transfer to a paper towel–lined plate to drain.

3   Add the baby portobello mushrooms to the skillet with the rendered bacon fat. Sauté until all of the moisture is released from the mushrooms.

4   Add the heavy cream, and then stir to combine. Add the garlic paste and Parmesan, stir again, and then bring to a light simmer. Cook until the sauce thickens, about 1 to 2 minutes.

5   Preheat the oven broiler.

6   Add the cooked gnocchi to the sauce. Simmer for another minute or two to allow the sauce to thicken.

7   Transfer the gnocchi and sauce to a large baking tray. Sprinkle the shredded Gouda over the top, and then place the gnocchi under the broiler until the cheese is fully melted, about 10 minutes. Transfer to a serving dish. Serve warm.

PAN-SEARED
FOIE GRAS

Foie gras, otherwise known as duck liver, is one of the most amazing delicacies in the world. It's absolutely delicious when thinly shaved over a nice, juicy steak. Give it a try! You won't regret it!

2 ½oz (71g) sliced and prepared foie gras (about 2 pieces)

LET'S DO IT!

1   Place a medium skillet over high heat. (You'll want the skillet to be really, *really* hot!)

2   Place the foie gras in the pan. Sauté, turning frequently, until it develops a nice crust on both sides.

3   Place the foie gras in the fridge to cool for at least 1 hour before shaving over the top of a steak (or whatever else you want to make more delicious).

GRILLED CHICKEN HEARTS

Yes, I know what you're thinking: "Chicken hearts? Eww!" But like the old saying goes: Don't knock it 'til you try it! This is a classic side in Brazil and can be found in most Brazilian steakhouses. If you're open to exploring new tastes, this recipe will absolutely change your mind. These are amazing!

1lb (454g) chicken hearts

½ medium white onion, diced

2 tbsp low-sodium soy sauce

1 tbsp chili crisp

Juice of 1 medium lemon

3 tbsp chopped fresh parsley

1 tbsp red wine vinegar

Coarse kosher salt

Ground black pepper

7–8 bamboo skewers

PREP AND SEASONING

1   Trim any excess fat from the hearts. Press the main arteries to remove any excess blood.

2   Place the hearts in a colander. Rinse at least twice under cold water to clean them well. Drain.

3   Place the chicken hearts in a large bowl. Add the onion, soy sauce, chili crisp, lemon juice, parsley, and red wine vinegar. Season the hearts liberally with kosher salt and black pepper. Toss to coat, and then cover and transfer to the fridge to marinate overnight.

4   Once the marinating time is complete, place the bamboo skewers in a large bowl filled with water. Allow to soak for 20 to 30 minutes, and then remove the skewers from the water.

5   Skewer the hearts onto the bamboo skewers. Discard the marinade.

TIP   *Chili crisp is a spicy condiment with a crunchy texture. You can find it in the specialty foods section of most grocery stores.*

LET'S DO IT!

1   Set up the grill for direct cooking. Preheat to 250°F (121°C).

2   Place the skewers on the grill. Cook, turning the skewers occasionally, until the hearts reach an internal temperature of 165°F (74°C), about 10 to 15 minutes.

3   Set aside to rest for 5 minutes. Serve hot!

BRAZILIAN
DEEP-FRIED BANANAS

You can find this inexpensive treat in Brazilian steakhouses or in any Brazilian household. If you want to eat these as an appetizer (like we do in Brazil), sprinkle some sugar and cinnamon over the top of the bananas while they're still hot. If you want to enjoy them as an extra-special dessert, melt some chocolate and then drizzle it over the top of the fried bananas.

3 cups vegetable oil

2 large eggs

½ cup all-purpose flour

½ cup plain unseasoned bread crumbs

3 ripe medium bananas

2 tbsp granulated sugar

1–2 tbsp ground cinnamon

LET'S DO IT!

1 Add the vegetable oil to a large, deep skillet over medium-high heat.

2 Place the eggs in a small bowl. Whisk to combine.

3 Place the flour in second small bowl.

4 Place the bread crumbs in a third small bowl. Set aside.

5 Peel the bananas, and then cut each into three equal-sized segments.

6 Dredge the banana segments in the flour, dip them in the egg wash, and then coat them in the bread crumbs. Place them on a plate.

7 When the oil is hot, add the banana segments in small batches. Shallow fry until they develop a nice golden-brown crust. Place the fried bananas on a paper towel–lined plate to drain. Repeat with the remaining banana segments.

8 Sprinkle the sugar and cinnamon over the top of the hot bananas. Shake gently to remove any excess. Serve warm.

SIDES & APPETIZERS

PÃO DE QUEIJO

From my hometown in Brazil, Uberaba, Minas Gerais, I bring you the world-famous Pão de Queijo, also known as Brazilian cheese bread. This bread is made in just about every Brazilian churrascaria (a Brazilian-style steak restaurant). It's easy to make and is really an amazing recipe!

2 cups whole milk

½ cup vegetable oil

5 cups tapioca starch

2 tsp fine table salt

2 large eggs

2 cups shredded mozzarella

1 cup grated Parmesan cheese

PREP AND SEASONING

1   Combine the milk and vegetable oil in a large saucepan over medium-high heat. Bring just to a boil, and then remove from the heat.

2   Combine the tapioca starch and salt in a large bowl or the bowl of a stand mixer.

3   Begin mixing the tapioca starch and salt with a hand mixer or stand mixer while slowly adding the milk–vegetable oil mixture. Add the eggs and continue mixing until the ingredients are combined.

4   Add the mozzarella and Parmesan cheeses. Stir until a dough is formed.

LET'S DO IT!

1   Preheat the oven to 325°F (163°C).

2   Line a large baking tray with aluminum foil. Spray a light layer of nonstick cooking spray onto the foil.

3   Using two spoons, form the dough into small balls, and then place the balls on the prepared baking tray.

4   Bake for 30 minutes or until lightly golden brown. (This bread will last up to 6 months in the freezer.)

ELOTE
(MEXICAN STREET CORN)

This is one of the most popular street foods in Mexico. Sometimes it's grilled and sometimes it's cooked on the stovetop, but either way, it's super easy to make. Try this recipe and you'll be thanking me later! The flavors are out of this world!

10 tbsp butter, divided

2 cups whole milk

4 ears sweet corn

2 tbsp mayonnaise

1 cup crumbled cotija cheese

Tajín Chile Lime Seasoning

1 small lime, cut into wedges

LET'S DO IT!

1   Set up the grill for direct cooking. Preheat to 450°F (232°C).

2   Place a large pot of water over medium-high heat. Add 8 tablespoons butter and the milk. Bring to a boil.

3   Add the corn to the pot. Cook until the corn is tender, about 10 to 15 minutes. (To check the doneness of the corn, insert a toothpick into a kernel. If the kernel snaps but feels soft inside, the corn is ready.)

4   Drain the ears and place them on the hot grill. Lightly char the ears, rotating them frequently, just until they develop nice color on all sides. (Don't overdo it! You just want to add a nice char. You can also add the char using a torch or by placing the ears over a stove-top burner.)

5   Transfer the ears to a cooling rack. Immediately rub the remaining butter over the entire surface of the ears.

6   Brush the mayonnaise over the entire surface of the ears, and then sprinkle the cotija cheese over the entire surface of the ears.

7   Lightly season the tops of the ears with the Tajín seasoning. (Be careful not to overdo it; the Tajín has a strong lime flavor.)

8   Serve with a lime wedge on the side for squeezing.

TIP *Tajín seasoning can be found in most Mexican grocery stores.*

DO IT LIKE GUGA!

If you want to take your elote to the next level, make a sofrito cooking sauce that you can drizzle over the top of the ears. To make the sofrito, add some oil to a hot skillet and then add ¼ cup diced white onion. Sauté over medium heat until the onion is browned. Add 1 seeded and diced red bell pepper, stir, and then cook for about 2 minutes more. Add 3 cloves minced garlic. Cook for another 2 minutes, and then add 2 tablespoons tomato paste. Mix well and then deglaze the pan with ½ cup beer. Simmer until the beer is evaporated. Next, add 1 tablespoon heavy cream, stir, and then season with salt and black pepper to taste. Spoon the sofrito over the ears just prior to serving. This is a game changer!

ROASTED GARLIC MASHED POTATOES

Roasted garlic is one of the most delicious flavors in the world. It's super easy to make and will really enhance the flavor of anything you add it to. It adds a sweet, mellow flavor that won't overpower the food but complement it perfectly. Give this one a try; you won't regret it!

1 large head garlic

Coarse kosher salt

Ground black pepper

1–2 tbsp olive oil

2lb (907g) Yukon Gold potatoes

8 tbsp butter (room temperature), divided

4 tbsp cream cheese

½ cup whole milk

2 cups seasoned panko bread crumbs

¼ cup grated Parmesan cheese

PREP AND SEASONING

1   Set up the grill for direct cooking. Preheat to 300°F (149°C).

2   Cut off the top of the garlic head. Season with kosher salt and black pepper. Place the head in a small sheet of aluminum foil and then drizzle some olive oil over the top. Wrap it up tightly.

3   Place the garlic head on the hot grill. Cook until the garlic is soft and golden, about 30 minutes to 1 hour, depending on the size of the garlic head.

LET'S DO IT!

1   Fill a large pot with water. Salt the water with a liberal amount of kosher salt, and then bring to a boil over medium-high heat.

2   Add the potatoes to the boiling water. Boil until the potatoes are fork tender, about 15 to 25 minutes. Drain.

3   Dice the potatoes and then process them through a potato ricer. (Alternatively, add them to a large bowl and mash them with a potato masher until there are no lumps.)

4   Add the potatoes to a food processor. Squeeze the garlic head to add the roasted garlic, and then add 4 tablespoons of the butter. Pulse until everything is well combined.

5   Add the cream cheese and milk. Continue pulsing until the ingredients are well combined and smooth. Season to taste with kosher salt and black pepper, and then transfer the mixture to a large baking dish. Set aside.

6   Preheat the oven broiler to high.

7   In a medium pan over medium heat, melt the remaining 4 tablespoons of butter and then add the bread crumbs. Stir to combine and then sauté until the bread crumbs are lightly toasted. Sprinkle the butter and bread crumbs over the potatoes, followed by the Parmesan.

8   Broil until the cheese is golden brown, about 3 to 5 minutes. (Watch carefully to ensure the cheese and bread crumbs do not burn.)

SALPICÃO

This dish can be found in every churrascaria in Brazil. It's one of the most famous salads in Brazil, and for good reason—it's absolutely delicious! You can pair it with any steak and have a delicious meal.

2 medium chicken breasts

Guga's BBQ Rub (p. 200)

2 (8.5oz/241g) cans green peas and diced carrots, drained

1 (8.5oz/241g) can corn kernels, drained

1 (8.5oz/241g) can diced beets, drained

½ cup mayonnaise

1 (7.6fl oz/225mL) can table cream

1 (9oz/255g) can shoestring potato sticks

PREP AND SEASONING

1   Liberally season the chicken breasts with Guga's BBQ Rub.

2   Combine the peas and carrots, corn, and beets in a medium bowl. Add the mayonnaise and table cream. Toss to combine. Cover with plastic wrap and place in the fridge until you're ready to serve.

LET'S DO IT!

1   Preheat the smoker to 250°F (121°C).

2   Place the chicken breasts in the smoker. Smoke until the chicken reaches an internal temperature of 165°F (74°C), about 30 to 45 minutes.

3   Remove the chicken from the smoker. Transfer to a cutting board to rest for 10 to 15 minutes.

4   Shred or finely dice the rested chicken, and then set it aside to cool. Once cooled, add the chicken to the vegetable mix. Toss to combine.

5   Top the salad with a generous sprinkling of the shoestring potato sticks.

COLESLAW

This coleslaw is so delicious and simple to make that you'll want to make it every time you barbecue! It's always a hit, particularly when it's paired with spicy, rich barbecue. And there's no need to do a bunch of chopping: you can simply use precut coleslaw mix and this recipe will still turn out absolutely amazing. Everyone is going to be begging you for this recipe!

1 cup mayonnaise

3 tbsp apple cider vinegar

1 tsp celery seed

3 tsp sugar

½ tbsp honey

Coarse kosher salt and ground black pepper, to taste

1 (16oz/454g) bag precut coleslaw mix

LET'S DO IT!

1   Combine the mayonnaise, apple cider vinegar, celery seed, sugar, and honey in a large bowl. Whisk to combine. Season to taste with kosher salt and black pepper.

2   Add the coleslaw mix to a large bowl.

3   Drizzle the dressing over the coleslaw mix. Toss to coat. Serve right away or refrigerate before serving.

GREEK SALAD

This salad is light and refreshing, and pairs perfectly with any dish. Make this for dinner or for a barbecue and watch how fast it disappears! If you're going to a large gathering, be sure to double or triple the recipe to ensure everyone's bellies will be happy.

5 mini cucumbers, diced

3 small red tomatoes, diced

½ cup crumbled feta cheese

¼ cup sliced black olives

½ cup thinly sliced carrots

1 tbsp finely chopped red onion

⅛ cup diced green onion

5 tbsp olive oil

2 tbsp red wine vinegar

Coarse kosher salt and ground black pepper, to taste

LET'S DO IT!

1   Combine the cucumbers, tomatoes, feta, black olives, carrots, red onion, green onion, olive oil, and red wine vinegar in a large bowl. Toss to combine.

2   Season to taste with kosher salt and black pepper.

SMOKED MAC AND CHEESE

Everyone loves mac and cheese and this one will be no different. The hints of smoky flavor from both the cheese and the smoker make this one amazing! And of course, you know it's going to be extra cheesy!

16oz (454g) box small shell pasta

3 tbsp butter

5 tbsp all-purpose flour

2 cups whole milk (plus more, if needed)

1 tsp ground nutmeg

4 tbsp cream cheese

2 cups shredded mild Cheddar cheese

1 cup shredded smoked Gouda cheese

Coarse kosher salt, to taste

1 cup shredded mozzarella

PREP AND SEASONING

1   Cook the pasta per package instructions. Drain and transfer to a large bowl. Set aside.

2   Begin making the cheese sauce by melting the butter in a medum saucepan over medium heat. Add the flour and cook until the mixture begins to smell like pie dough.

3   Add the milk, whisking continuously until the sauce thickens. Add the nutmeg, cream cheese, Cheddar, and smoked Gouda. Stir continuously until the cheese is fully melted. (Add additional milk in small amounts if the sauce becomes too thick.)

LET'S DO IT!

1   Preheat the smoker to 350°F (177°C).

2   Add the sauce to the bowl with the pasta, and then toss to coat. Season to taste with kosher salt.

3   Transfer the mixture to a large baking dish. Sprinkle the mozzarella over the top.

4   Place the dish in the smoker. Smoke until the cheese is nice and melted, about 30 minutes. Serve warm.

PICKLED KOREAN CUCUMBERS

These pickled cucumbers are the perfect topping for a sandwich or just to enjoy as a quick snack. They are easy to make and super delicious. The best part is that you can change it up and make them your own!

2 large Korean cucumbers
2 cups water
1 cup red wine vinegar
1 tbsp Korean chili flakes

LET'S DO IT!

1   Slice the cucumbers thin, but not too thin. Transfer the slices to a large heat-safe jar or bowl. Set aside.

2   Combine the water, vinegar, and chili flakes in a large pot. Bring to a boil over medium-high heat.

3   Once the brine reaches a boil, pour it over the cucumbers. Allow to cool slightly, and then cover the container tightly.

4   Set the cucumbers aside to cool completely, and then transfer to the fridge. Refrigerate for up to 5 days.

DO IT LIKE GUGA!

You can add any spices you like to the brine. I like to add coarse black pepper or mustard seeds.

GARLIC BREAD

This homemade garlic bread is way better than the store-bought frozen stuff! If you're going to make an amazing main dish, the side has to match it, and this addicting bread will be the perfect complement to whatever you cook. Once you try this recipe, you'll never make garlic bread any other way!

4 tbsp Wagyu tallow

10 garlic cloves

8 tbsp soft Irish butter (I like Kerrygold brand)

1 tbsp chopped Italian flat-leaf parsley

1 tbsp lemon zest

1 loaf ciabatta bread, split lengthwise

4 tbsp grated Parmesan cheese

LET'S DO IT!

1   Preheat the oven to 350°F (177°C).

2   Add the Wagyu tallow to an oven-safe bowl. Place the bowl in the oven, and allow the tallow to melt completely.

3   Once the tallow is melted, add the garlic cloves to the bowl. Roast until the garlic is soft and golden, about 30 minutes.

4   Once the garlic is roasted, remove the bowl from the oven and add the garlic cloves and tallow to a food processor along with the butter. Process until the ingredients are well combined and smooth.

5   Add the parsley and lemon zest. Process again until smooth, and then place the garlic butter in the fridge to firm up for about 30 minutes to 1 hour.

6   Once the butter has firmed up, spread it over the split sides of the bread loaf and then sprinkle the Parmesan over the top of the butter.

7   Place the bread halves on a large baking sheet. Transfer to the oven and bake until the cheese is golden brown, about 5 to 10 minutes.

PICKLED RED ONIONS

These onions are the perfect way to add some extra flavor to any BBQ dish. (Add these to a pulled pork sandwich for some acidity, and see how much better the sandwich tastes.) You can even eat them on their own as a side. You'll love these!

2 medium red onions

2 cups red wine vinegar

2 tbsp granulated sugar

2 tbsp allspice berries

1 tsp mustard seeds

1 tsp ground black pepper

LET'S DO IT!

1   Thick slice the onions. Transfer to a large heat-safe jar or bowl. Set aside.

2   Add the vinegar, sugar, allspice berries, mustard seeds, and black pepper to a medium pot. Bring to a boil over medium-high heat.

3   Once the brine reaches a boil, pour it over the onions. Allow to cool slightly, and then cover the container tightly.

4   Set the onions aside to cool completely, and then transfer to the fridge. Refrigerate for up to 5 days.

TIP *If you prefer a brine that is milder and less red, add 2 cups water to the brine.*

JAPANESE POTATO SALAD

This side dish is perfect served alongside fatty meats because it helps cut the richness of the fat. (I highly recommend making this side dish if you are serving fatty cuts like ribeye.) Japanese mayonnaise is used because of the unique flavor profile it adds to the salad.

1 medium carrot, peeled and diced

1 medium cucumber, thinly sliced

½ medium white onion, thinly sliced

Coarse kosher salt

5 medium Yukon Gold potatoes, peeled and cut into large cubes

Ground black pepper

4 tbsp Japanese mayonnaise (I like Kewpie brand)

5 slices prosciutto, diced

1 (4oz/113g) can shoestring potatoes

1 tbsp chopped fresh parsley

PREP AND SEASONING

1   Fill a small saucepan with water and place it over medium-high heat. Bring to a boil.

2   Place the carrots in the water. Boil until soft, about 4 minutes. Drain and set aside.

3   Place the cucumbers and onion in separate bowls. Season the cucumbers liberally with coarse kosher salt, and then add enough water to both bowls to cover the ingredients. Set aside.

TIP   *For best results, I recommend using a mandoline slicer for slicing the cucumbers and onions.*

LET'S DO IT!

1   Fill a large pot with water and place it over medium-high heat. Add the potatoes and boil until tender but not soft, about 15 minutes. Drain.

2   Use a wooden spoon to mash the potatoes just a bit. (Don't mash the potatoes completely; you just want to break the potatoes into smaller chunks.) Season liberally with kosher salt and black pepper.

3   Thoroughly drain the onions and cucumbers, removing as much liquid as possible.

4   Add the carrots, cucumbers, and onions to the bowl with the potatoes. Mix well to combine.

5   Add the mayonnaise and prosciutto. Mix well. (You can add more mayo if you like. This is all about personal preference.)

6   Sprinkle the shoestring potatoes over the top, and then sprinkle the parsley over the top. (This is delicious served either warm or cold.)

TIP   *You can make this a day ahead and keep it in the refrigerator. Just be sure to cover it with plastic wrap, and don't add the shoestring potatoes until you are ready to serve.*

SMOKED JALAPEÑO POPPERS

These smoked poppers are so easy to make and everyone will love them, even those who don't like jalapeños! Trust me, these aren't spicy; the jalapeños just produce an incredible flavor that is impossible to replace.

---

2 medium chorizo sausages

8 tbsp cream cheese (about half an 8oz/227g block)

1 cup shredded Cheddar cheese

4 garlic cloves, minced

1 tbsp minced shallots

8 jalapeños

2 tbsp avocado oil

½ lb (227g) bacon (about 8 strips), cut in half

Guga's BBQ Rub (p. 200)

FOR THE SWEET GLAZE

4 tbsp honey

4 tbsp maple syrup

2 tbsp sauerkraut

1 tbsp bourbon

PREP AND SEASONING

1 Remove and discard the casings from the sausages. Set the meat aside.

2 Combine the cream cheese, Cheddar cheese, garlic, and shallots in a food processor. Process until a paste is formed. Set aside.

3 Remove the stems from the jalapeños, and then cut them in half lengthwise. Use a paring knife to remove the pith (white part) and the seeds.

TIP *Be sure to make a lot of these because there is never enough! You can easily double or triple this recipe. And if you don't have a smoker, you can just pop them under the broiler and they'll still be amazing!*

LET'S DO IT!

1 Preheat the smoker to 325°F (163°C).

2 Add the avocado oil to a large skillet over medium-high heat. Add the sausage to the skillet and use a wooden spoon to break the sausage into small pieces. Cook until the sausage is browned and cooked through. Transfer to a paper towel–lined plate to drain.

3 Stuff a jalapeño with the cream cheese mixture, add some of the chorizo, and then wrap the pepper with a slice of bacon. Repeat with the remaining peppers and then season the peppers liberally with Guga's BBQ Rub. Place the stuffed peppers on a small baking tray.

4 Place the peppers in the smoker. Smoke for 30 minutes or until the bacon is fully cooked.

5 While the peppers are smoking, begin making the glaze. Preheat a pan over medium heat. Add the honey and maple syrup, stir, and then reduce the heat to low. Once the mixture begins to bubble, add the sauerkraut, stir, and then add the bourbon. Cook until the alcohol is burned off, about 5 minutes. (You can also light the mixture with a torch lighter to burn off the alcohol, just be careful not to burn yourself. Once all the alcohol is burned off, the flames will extinguish.)

6 Drizzle the glaze over the top of the poppers. Serve warm.

SHORT RIB
POTATOES AU GRATIN

This is a staple side dish in any good steakhouse! That's where I became addicted to it. It's so easy to make at home; once you do it, you'll never want to stop!

5lb (2.25kg) short ribs

Coarse kosher salt

Ground black pepper

Garlic powder

6 large russet potatoes

½ large white onion

1 cup heavy cream

2 tbsp minced garlic

12 strips bacon

2 tbsp chopped fresh parsley

2 cups grated Parmesan cheese

PREP AND SEASONING

1 Remove the silver skin and cap fat from the short ribs. (Doing this will enable you to season them better.) Liberally season the ribs with kosher salt, black pepper, and garlic powder. Set aside.

2 Add enough water to a large bowl to cover the potatoes. Peel the potatoes, and then use a mandoline slicer or food processor to slice the potatoes into thin slices. Place the slices in the water. Set aside.

3 Using a box grater, grate the onion and then squeeze it in paper towels to remove as much of the moisture as possible.

4 Combine the grated onion, heavy cream, and garlic in a medium bowl. Season to taste with kosher salt and black pepper.

5 Drain the potatoes thoroughly, and then pour the sauce over the top of the potatoes. Gently toss to coat, ensuring every slice is coated with the sauce. Transfer to the fridge while you get the smoker ready.

LET'S DO IT!

1 Preheat the smoker to 250°F (121°C).

2 Place the ribs in the smoker. Cook for about 4 hours or until the ribs develop a nice mahogany color.

3 After 4 hours, take the ribs out of the smoker, wrap them in aluminum foil, and place them back in the smoker. Continue smoking until the internal temperature reaches 175°F (79°C) and an instant-read thermometer inserted into the ribs goes in like a knife through room-temperature butter, about 2 to 4 hours.

4 While the ribs are cooking, add the bacon strips to a large skillet over medium heat. Cook until the bacon is fully cooked and the fat has been rendered. Transfer to a paper towel–lined plate to drain, and then chop into small pieces. Set aside.

5 When the ribs are done cooking, remove them from the smoker and transfer them to a cutting board. Use a sharp boning knife to cut the meat from the bones, and then shred the meat.

6 Preheat the oven to 400°F (204°C).

7 Add about a third of the potatoes in a layer into the bottom of a large cast-iron pan, followed by about a third of the chopped bacon, followed by about a third of the shredded rib meat. Continue layering the ingredients, and then top the potatoes with the parsley. Cover the pan with aluminum foil.

8 Bake 1 hour and then remove the pan from the oven. Adjust the oven to the broil setting.

9 Remove the foil and sprinkle the Parmesan over the top. Place the pan back in the oven, uncovered, and broil until the cheese is golden brown. Serve hot.

TWICE-LOADED
SWEET POTATOES

There are so many different ways to cook sweet potatoes, but I guarantee this one will be a favorite every time. Even if you don't like sweet potatoes, I encourage you to give this recipe a try! (This recipe works for any baking potato, so you can also use russet potatoes, if you prefer.)

4 large sweet potatoes

½ lb (227g) diced uncooked bacon (about 10 strips)

1 (8oz/227g) package plus 4 tbsp cream cheese

1 cup shredded mozzarella, divided

1 cup shredded Cheddar cheese

Coarse kosher salt

Ground black pepper

1 cup sour cream

1 tbsp chopped fresh chives

PREP AND SEASONING

1   Preheat the oven to 400°F (204°C).

2   Place the sweet potatoes directly on the middle rack in the oven. Bake for 1 hour or until a knife can be easily inserted into a potato.

3   While the potatoes are baking, place a medium skillet over medium heat. Add the bacon and fry until it's nice and crispy. Transfer the bacon to a paper towel–lined plate to drain. Transfer the rendered fat to a heat-proof container. Set aside. Divide the bacon into two equal-sized portions.

4   Once the potatoes are done baking, transfer them to a cutting board. Using a sharp knife, carefully cut the tops from the potatoes. Use a spoon to scoop out the flesh, being very careful to not break the skins. Place the flesh in a large bowl, and then set the skins aside.

5   Combine the potato flesh, reserved bacon fat, cream cheese, half of the shredded mozzarella, and the shredded Cheddar cheese in a food processor. Process until the ingredients are smooth and creamy. Season to taste with kosher salt and black pepper, and then scoop the filling back into the potato skins. Top the potatoes with the remaining mozzarella and half of the bacon pieces.

LET'S DO IT!

1   Adjust the oven setting to broil. Place the loaded potatoes on a large baking tray, and place them back in the oven. Broil until the cheese is fully melted, about 5 minutes.

2   Top each potato with 4 tablespoons sour cream, and then top with the remaining bacon pieces. Sprinkle the chopped chives over the top. Serve hot.

TIP *The potatoes can be prepared and filled ahead of time and just finished in the oven whenever you are ready to serve. Just be sure to wrap them with plastic wrap and place them in the refrigerator so they don't dry out.*

BREAD BACON BITES

These tender bites are perfect paired with steak or any other meat. Make them for a holiday feast or fight night and watch them disappear just as quickly as you put them out. These are so easy to make and incredibly delicious!

1lb (454g) block low-moisture mozzarella cheese

1 (16oz/454g) can buttermilk biscuits

1lb (454g) center-cut bacon (about 16 strips)

4 cups canola oil (for frying)

FOR THE SPICY MAYO DIPPING SAUCE

3 tbsp mayonnaise

1 tbsp sriracha

1 tsp honey

1 tsp minced fresh parsley

1 tsp garlic paste

PREP AND SEASONING

1   Make the spicy mayo dipping sauce by combining the mayonnaise, sriracha, honey, parsley, and garlic paste in a medium bowl. Mix well and then cover. Transfer to the fridge until you are ready to serve.

2   Cut the mozzarella block into 16 1-inch (2.5cm) cubes.

3   Remove the biscuits from the can. Separate into 8 biscuits and then use a sharp knife to slice the biscuits into 16 thinner biscuits. Spread the biscuits out in a single layer on a cutting board.

4   Add 1 cheese cube to the middle of a biscuit. Pinch the biscuit shut to form a ball, and then wrap a piece of bacon around the ball. Stick a toothpick through the center to secure the ball. Repeat with the remaining ingredients.

LET'S DO IT!

1   Add the canola oil to a large skillet over medium-high heat. Heat the oil to 325°F (163°C).

2   Carefully place the dough balls in the hot oil. Fry until the bacon fat fully renders and the bread is cooked all the way through, while constantly moving the balls and basting them with the hot oil so they cook evenly, about 5 to 10 minutes.

3   Transfer the fried bites to a paper towel-lined plate to drain. Serve with the spicy mayo dipping sauce on the side.

SIMPLE VINAIGRETTE SALAD

This is the definition of a perfect side dish. It's a nice light salad with some acidity from the vinegar. This dish helps keep everything fresh, while also providing a lot of flavor. This one is a must-make!

1 large white onion, finely diced

4 large red tomatoes, seeded and finely diced

1 medium green bell pepper, seeded and finely diced

⅓ cup chopped fresh parsley

¼ cup red wine vinegar

½ cup avocado oil

Coarse kosher salt and ground black pepper, to taste

LET'S DO IT!

1   Combine the ingredients in a medium bowl. Mix well and then season to taste with kosher salt and black pepper.

2   Transfer to an airtight container. Store in the fridge for 1 to 2 days.

SAUCES, RUBS & SEASONINGS

GUGA'S BBQ RUB

This is a great basic seasoning that will make anything you cook delicious. This is an inexpensive rub to make, so make lots of it so you can always have it handy for all of your cooks!

¼ cup coarse kosher salt

¼ cup smoked paprika

1 tbsp garlic powder

1 tbsp onion powder

1 tbsp ground black pepper

1 tbsp turmeric

1 tsp ground cinnamon

LET'S DO IT!

1   Combine the kosher salt, smoked paprika, garlic powder, onion powder, black pepper, turmeric, and ground cinnamon in a medium bowl.

2   Mix well to combine.

3   Transfer to an airtight container. Store in a cool, dry place.

TIP   *To make a salt-free version of the rub, simply omit the coarse kosher salt. (It will still be delicious!)*

GUGA'S BBQ SAUCE

What's good barbecue without a really good BBQ sauce? This sauce pairs perfectly with everything—from ribs to chicken to pulled pork. It will make whatever you cook an absolute hit!

1½ cups ketchup

1 cup brown sugar

¼ cup molasses

¼ cup water

1 tbsp Worcestershire sauce

1 tsp liquid smoke

¼ cup pineapple juice

1 tbsp paprika

2 tsp garlic powder

1 tbsp dry mustard

1 tsp ground black pepper

1 tsp coarse kosher salt

Sriracha sauce, to taste (optional)

LET'S DO IT!

1 Combine the ketchup, brown sugar, molasses, water, Worcestershire sauce, liquid smoke, pineapple juice, paprika, garlic powder, dry mustard, black pepper, and kosher salt in a large saucepan over low heat.

2 Simmer, stirring frequently, until the sauce reduces to a thick sauce-like consistency, about 10 minutes. Add sriracha sauce (if using) to taste.

3 Allow to cool completely before transferring to an airtight container. Store in the fridge for 3 to 4 weeks.

BUTTER OF THE GODS

"Butter of the Gods" has its name for a reason. It's a combination of delicious ingredients that will take any steak over the top. This really is as good as it gets!

½ gallon (1.90L) water

½ cup fine table salt

2 beef bone marrow canoes

8 tbsp butter

1 Cured Egg Yolk (p. 203)

1 tsp minced fresh parsley

2 tsp minced shallots

1 tsp anchovy paste

1 tsp coarse kosher salt

LET'S DO IT!

1   Combine the water and fine table salt in a medium bowl. Stir until the salt is fully dissolved.

2   Place the bone marrow canoes in the water. Transfer to the fridge to soak for at least 24 hours and up to 3 days. (This process removes the blood from the marrow. The longer you leave the bones in the water, the more blood will be extracted.)

3   Once the blood is extracted from the bone marrow, remove the canoes from the water and pat them dry with paper towels.

4   Preheat the broiler on its highest setting. Place the bone marrow canoes on a baking tray. Place them in the oven to broil for 10 minutes.

5   When the canoes are done broiling, remove them from the oven. Allow to cool slightly and use a spoon to scrape the bone marrow into a bowl.

6   Add the bone marrow to a food processor along with the butter, Cured Egg Yolk, parsley, shallots, anchovy paste, and kosher salt. Process until well combined.

7   Place the mixture on a sheet of plastic wrap and then roll it up tightly. Place it in the fridge to solidify for at least 1 hour.

8   Slice the butter and then place it atop a beautifully cooked steak!

CURED EGG YOLKS

Sprinkle these yolks over a nice juicy steak and you'll thank me later! Just keep them handy for whenever you want to add an extra layer of flavor to a dish and impress your guests! You can grate them over steaks or even pasta.

1 dozen large eggs
2lb (907g) fine table salt
2lb (907g) granulated sugar

LET'S DO IT!

1. Separate the egg yolks from the egg whites. Carefully place the yolks in a medium bowl and discard the whites. (Be very careful not to break the yolks.)

2. Combine the salt and sugar in a medium bowl. Stir until well combined.

3. Pour half of the salt-sugar mixture onto a large plate. Use the back of a spoon to make a small divot in each of the yolks. Carefully place the yolks on the plate and on top of the salt-sugar mixture.

4. Cover the yolks with the remaining salt-sugar mixture. Transfer to the fridge to cure, uncovered, for 5 to 7 days.

5. After the curing time is complete, remove the yolks from the fridge, and then use a spoon to carefully remove them from the salt-sugar mixture. Very gently rinse the yolks under cool water to remove any remaining salt-sugar mixture.

6. Place the yolks on a baking tray lined with parchment paper.

7. Preheat the oven to 150°F (66°C) or the lowest setting. Place the tray with the yolks in the oven, and bake for 2 hours or until the yolks are fully dried.

8. After 2 hours, remove the yolks from the oven. Store in an airtight container in the fridge for up to 3 months.

PINEAPPLE SAUCE

This sauce is a little bit different, but super good. It goes well with fish tacos, pulled pork sandwiches, or even burgers. It's light and fresh, and will add some amazing flavor to your dish!

2 tbsp olive oil

1 garlic clove, minced

1 tbsp minced shallots

3 tbsp butter

½ cup heavy cream

¼ cup crushed pineapple (fresh or canned)

LET'S DO IT!

1 Add the olive oil to a medium skillet over medium heat.

2 Add the garlic and shallots to the skillet. Sauté until lightly browned, and then add the butter, heavy cream, and crushed pineapple. (If using canned pineapple, be sure to drain it before adding it to the skillet.)

3 Simmer until the sauce reduces to a syrup-like consistency, about 10 minutes. Drizzle warm over burgers, tacos, or sandwiches.

GREEK YOGURT

HORSE-RADISH SAUCE

This creamy horseradish sauce is perfect paired with a juicy steak. It has a nice tangy flavor that keeps everything fresh, and is a step up from traditional horseradish sauce.

½ cup sour cream

1 cup plain Greek yogurt

2 tbsp prepared horseradish

1 tbsp lemon juice

2 tbsp finely chopped fresh chives

Coarse kosher salt and ground black pepper, to taste

LET'S DO IT!

1 Combine the sour cream, Greek yogurt, prepared horseradish, lemon juice, and chives in a medium bowl.

2 Stir to combine. Season to taste with kosher salt and black pepper.

3 Transfer to an airtight container. Store in the fridge for up to 1 week.

BIRRIA TACOS RED SAUCE

For those who do not fear spice and really enjoy amazing flavors, this sauce is for you. Birria tacos are already one of the best foods in the world, and adding this sauce makes them even better. If you're going to take the time to make these incredible tacos, do yourself a favor and make this sauce to go with them.

2 tbsp olive oil

10 tomatillos, husks and stems removed

3 garlic cloves

½ medium white onion, diced

20 arbol chiles

3 tbsp chopped fresh cilantro

Coarse kosher salt and ground black pepper, to taste

LET'S DO IT!

1   Place a large skillet over medium-high heat. Add the olive oil.

2   When the oil is hot, add the tomatillos to the skillet. Roast until the tomatillos develop a nice char, about 5 minutes, and then remove them from the pan.

3   Add the garlic cloves, onion, and chilis to the same pan. Roast until they become fragrant and begin to brown.

4   Combine the tomatillos, garlic cloves, onion, chilis, and cilantro in a blender. Blend until well combined. Season to taste with kosher salt and black pepper.

5   Transfer to an airtight container. Store in the fridge for up to 1 week.

BIRRIA TACOS GREEN SAUCE

Birria tacos are absolutely amazing, and topping them with this sauce will make them to die for. This light, refreshing sauce is the perfect pairing with some amazing birria tacos.

2 tbsp olive oil

10 tomatillos, husks and stems removed

2 garlic cloves

1 serrano pepper

3 tbsp chopped fresh cilantro

2 medium avocados, diced

Coarse kosher salt and ground black pepper, to taste

LET'S DO IT!

1 Place a large skillet over medium-high heat. Add the olive oil.

2 When the oil is hot, add the tomatillos to the skillet. Roast until they develop a nice char, about 5 minutes, and then remove them from the pan.

3 Add the garlic cloves and serrano pepper to the same pan. Roast until the garlic cloves begin to brown and become fragrant.

4 Combine the tomatillos, garlic cloves, and serrano pepper in a blender with the cilantro and avocados. Blend until well combined. Season to taste with kosher salt and black pepper.

5 Transfer to an airtight container. Store in the fridge for up to 1 week.

RED TACO SAUCE

Every taco needs a good sauce, and this one is always an absolute go-to for me. It's a nice, creamy sauce that will make taco night a hit at your house every time!

1 medium red bell pepper

2 tbsp olive oil

½ medium white onion, diced

3 garlic cloves, minced

1 cup water

1 cube chicken bouillon

Juice of 1 medium lime

1 tbsp red wine vinegar

1 tbsp apple cider vinegar

1 tbsp Mexican crema

4 tbsp sour cream

Coarse kosher salt and ground black pepper, to taste

LET'S DO IT!

1   Char the surface of the bell pepper over an open flame on the stove top. Remove the seeds and then roughly chop. Set aside.

2   Add the olive oil to a medium pan over medium heat. When the oil is hot, add the onion and cook until translucent. Add the garlic and sauté until caramelized.

3   Add the water to deglaze the pan, and then add the bouillon cube. Reduce the heat to low. Simmer until the bouillon cube is fully dissolved. Stir.

4   Combine the bell pepper, onion and garlic mixture, lime juice, red wine vinegar, apple cider vinegar, Mexican crema, and sour cream in a blender. Blend until smooth and no chunks remain. Season with kosher salt and black pepper to taste.

5   Transfer to an airtight container. Store in the fridge for up to 1 week.

SPICY RED TACO SAUCE

This sauce is for those who like to live on the edge! If you want to take this sauce to the next level and really test your spice tolerance, keep the seeds from the chiles in the sauce!

5 dried arbol chiles

2 tomatillos, husks and stems removed

2 tbsp mayonnaise

1 tsp coarse kosher salt

1 tsp ground black pepper

LET'S DO IT!

1   Fill a medium saucepan halfway with water. Bring to a boil over medium-high heat.

2   Add the chiles to the boiling water. Boil until the chiles are soft and rehydrated.

3   Remove the chiles from the water and place them on a cutting board. Wearing food-safe gloves, use a sharp paring knife to spilt the chiles open. Gently scrape the insides with the knife to remove the seeds. (If you prefer your sauce *really* spicy, leave the seeds intact!) Set aside.

4   Char the tomatillos over an open flame on the stove top. Cut them into halves.

5   Combine the chiles, tomatillos, mayonnaise, kosher salt, and black pepper in a blender. Blend until everything is well combined and no lumps remain.

6   Transfer to an airtight container. Store in the fridge for up to 1 week.

TIP *Always wear food-safe gloves when removing the seeds from the chiles. Trust me, you don't want to touch your eyes after removing the seeds from these chiles!*

GREEN CHIMICHURRI SAUCE

This is the ultimate topping for a nice skirt steak! It features a good balance of freshness with just a little kick. This will have your taste buds dancing and have you coming back for more!

1 tbsp diced white onion

1 tbsp red wine vinegar

¼ cup chopped fresh parsley

½ tsp minced garlic

½ tsp chili flakes

½ tsp coarse kosher salt

½ tsp ground black pepper

1 tbsp olive oil

Juice of ½ medium lime

LET'S DO IT!

1 Combine the onion, red wine vinegar, parsley, garlic, chili flakes, kosher salt, black pepper, olive oil, and lime juice in a blender.

2 Blend until smooth and a sauce-like consistency is achieved.

3 Transfer to an airtight container. Store in the fridge for up to 2 months.

RED CHIMICHURRI SAUCE

This red chimichurri sauce is the definition of flavor. It's perfect drizzled over skirt steak or simply served as a dip for chips. The flavor is just mouthwatering. Once you try it, you'll understand what I mean!

4 tbsp roasted red bell peppers

2 tbsp chopped fresh parsley

2 tbsp chopped fresh cilantro

2 tbsp diced shallots

1 tbsp minced garlic

2 tbsp dried oregano

1 tsp coarse kosher salt

4 tbsp red wine vinegar

1 tsp ground black pepper

1 tbsp olive oil

3 tbsp avocado oil

2 tbsp lemon juice (optional)

LET'S DO IT!

1   Combine the bell peppers, parsley, cilantro, shallots, garlic, oregano, kosher salt, red wine vinegar, black pepper, olive oil, avocado oil, and lemon juice (if using) in a blender. (If you prefer the sauce be a little more tangy, add the lemon juice; if not, omit it.)

2   Blend until smooth and a sauce-like consistency is achieved.

3   Transfer to an airtight container. Store in the fridge for up to 2 months.

SPICY MAYO

Add this spicy mayo to any sandwich to take it to the next level. This is a very simple recipe, but it provides a crazy amount of flavor and kick. It's just perfect!

8 tbsp mayonnaise
1 tbsp sriracha sauce
½ tbsp honey

LET'S DO IT!

1   Combine the mayonnaise, sriracha sauce, and honey in a small bowl.

2   Mix until well combined.

3   Transfer to an airtight container. Store in the fridge for up to 1 week.

GARLIC CILANTRO MAYO

This mayo has a nice, fresh, earthy flavor. It can be used as a topping for tacos or sandwiches, or just enjoyed as a dip for potato chips. This sauce is crazy easy to make and will become one of your favorites!

1 large egg

1 tbsp lemon juice

1 tsp Dijon mustard

3 garlic cloves

1 cup avocado oil

¼ cup chopped fresh cilantro

Coarse kosher salt and ground black pepper, to taste

LET'S DO IT!

1 Combine the egg, lemon juice, Dijon mustard, garlic cloves, avocado oil, and cilantro in a large bowl.

2 Using an immersion blender, blend until the egg and oil emulsify and everything is well combined. Season to taste with kosher salt and black pepper.

3 Transfer to an airtight container. Store in the fridge for up to 1 week.

GUGA'S BASIC BURGER SAUCE

This burger sauce is super easy to make and will take your burgers to the next level! It's sweet, creamy, and bold, and will go perfectly with that nice, juicy cheeseburger! (This just happens to be my nephew's favorite burger topping.)

2 tbsp ketchup
2 tbsp mayonnaise
½ tbsp yellow mustard
1 tbsp Worcestershire sauce

LET'S DO IT!

1 Combine the ketchup, mayonnaise, yellow mustard, and Worcestershire sauce in a small bowl.

2 Mix well to combine.

3 Transfer to an airtight container. Store in the fridge for up to 1 week.

GUGA'S SPICY BURGER SAUCE

A burger is just a burger without fresh toppings and a nice burger sauce, and this recipe is for those who like a little extra kick in their sauce. It's a little spicy and a little sweet, which is the perfect flavor combination for a beautiful, juicy burger!

2 tbsp ketchup
2 tbsp mayonnaise
½ tbsp yellow mustard
1 tbsp Worcestershire sauce
½ tbsp balsamic vinegar
1 tbsp sriracha sauce

LET'S DO IT!

1 Combine the ketchup, mayonnaise, yellow mustard, Worcestershire sauce, balsamic vinegar, and sriracha sauce in a medium bowl.

2 Mix until well combined.

3 Transfer to an airtight container. Store in the fridge for up to 1 week.

DORITOS DUST

I've cracked the code! I've created a seasoning that captures that amazing, cheesy Doritos flavor that everyone loves. It's perfect for seasoning steaks or even making your own homemade Doritos!

1 cup powdered Cheddar cheese

¼ cup powdered white Cheddar cheese

2 tbsp powdered Romano cheese

¼ cup powdered buttermilk

2 tbsp nutritional yeast

1 tsp Homemade MSG Seasoning (p. 217) or store-bought MSG seasoning

2 tsp smoked paprika

1 tbsp onion powder

LET'S DO IT!

1 Combine the powdered Cheddar cheese, powdered white Cheddar cheese, powdered Romano cheese, powdered buttermilk, nutritional yeast, Homemade MSG Seasoning, smoked paprika, and onion powder in a large bowl.

2 Mix until the ingredients are well combined.

3 Transfer to an airtight container. Store in the fridge for up to 1 month.

BACON SALT

It's true! Bacon really does make everything better, and salt is the key to flavor. Combining these two ingredients is a match made in Heaven! Sprinkle some of this on a steak, and your tastebuds will thank you!

¼ lb (113g) uncooked bacon
(about 4 strips)

1 lb (454g) fine table salt

LET'S DO IT!

1   Place the bacon in a cold skillet. Turn the burner up to medium-high.

2   Cook the bacon until it's very crispy and almost all of the fat is rendered. Transfer the bacon to a paper towel–lined plate to drain.

3   Pat the bacon dry with additional paper towels. (You'll want to remove as much of the rendered fat as possible.) Crumble the bacon into small pieces.

4   Combine the crumbled bacon and salt in a food processer. Process until the ingredients reach a fine consistency.

5   Transfer to an airtight container. Store in the fridge for up to 2 weeks.

TIP *Don't just stop at bacon! You can make flavored salts using coffee, cured egg yolks, and even dried truffles. The possibilities are endless!*

HOMEMADE
MSG
SEASONING

MSG is considered to be the king of all flavors. And adding this homemade MSG seasoning to anything you cook will intensify the flavor and take it to heights you didn't think were possible—especially on a nice juicy steak!

4 large red tomatoes, thinly sliced

2 (2oz/57g) tins anchovies, drained

1 large white onion, thinly sliced

2 cups baby portobello mushrooms, thinly sliced

1 cup roughly diced Parmesan cheese

3–4 sheets kombu (dried sea kelp)

1 tbsp garlic powder

LET'S DO IT!

1　Layer the tomato slices, anchovies, onion slices, mushroom slices, and Parmesan chunks in separate trays in a food dehydrator. Dehydrate for 20 hours or until the ingredients are completely dried.

2　Once the dehydrating time is complete, individually process each of the dehydrated ingredients in a food processor until a fine powder is formed.

3　Process the kombu sheets in a food processor until a fine powder is formed.

4　Combine 1 tablespoon of each of the dehydrated ingredients in a medium bowl along with 1 tablespoon of the kombu powder and the garlic powder. Stir until the ingredients are well combined.

5　Transfer the seasoning to an airtight container. Store at room temperature for up to 2 weeks.

INDEX